Neither Yavne nor Antioch

Neither Yavne nor Antioch:

Recovering Nazarean Judaism

JOEL HELLER

RESOURCE *Publications* • Eugene, Oregon

NEITHER YAVNE NOR ANTIOCH
Recovering Nazarean Judaism

Copyright © 2022 Joel Heller. All rights reserved. Except for brief quotations in critical publications or reviews, no part of this book may be reproduced in any manner without prior written permission from the publisher. Write: Permissions, Wipf and Stock Publishers, 199 W. 8th Ave., Suite 3, Eugene, OR 97401.

Resource Publications
An Imprint of Wipf and Stock Publishers
199 W. 8th Ave., Suite 3
Eugene, OR 97401

www.wipfandstock.com

PAPERBACK ISBN: 978-1-6667-3448-5
HARDCOVER ISBN: 978-1-6667-9037-5
EBOOK ISBN: 978-1-6667-9038-2

JANUARY 7, 2022 10:11 AM

Unless otherwise noted, all scriptures are from the KING JAMES VERSION, public domain.

Scripture quotations marked (NIV) are taken from the Holy Bible, New International Version®, NIV®. Copyright © 1973, 1978, 1984, 2011 by Biblica, Inc.™ Used by permission of Zondervan. All rights reserved worldwide. www.zondervan.com. The "NIV" and "New International Version" are trademarks registered in the United States Patent and Trademark Office by Biblica, Inc.™

Scripture quotations marked (NIrV) are taken from the Holy Bible, New International Reader's Version®, NIrV® Copyright © 1995, 1996, 1998, 2014 by Biblica, Inc.™ Used by permission of Zondervan. All rights reserved worldwide. www.zondervan.com. The "NIrV" and "New International Reader's Version" are trademarks registered in the United States Patent and Trademark Office by Biblica, Inc.™

Scripture quotations marked (NLT) are taken from the Holy Bible, New Living Translation, copyright ©1996, 2004, 2015 by Tyndale House Foundation. Used by permission of Tyndale House Publishers, Carol Stream, Illinois 60188. All rights reserved.

Scripture quotations marked WNT are taken from the Weymouth New Testament (The New Testament in Modern Speech).

Prove all things; hold fast that which is good.
—1 Thessalonians 5:21

Go home. Read your Bible.
— Zachary Bauer

Contents

Acknowledgments | ix

Preface | xi

    Introduction | 1

    Methodology | 5

    Misunderstood Teachings | 17

    Human History | 21

    The Cousins | 26

    Lost Sheep | 28

    The Nazareans | 35

    Moses' Seat | 41

    Takanot Violated | 49

    Nazarean Lifestyle | 55

    Christian Drift | 58

    Departures from Apostles' Doctrine | 79

    Re-Examining Misconstrued Passages in Light of Hebrew Reasoning | 88

    Reformations | 112

    Conclusion | 122

Appendix 1: Baptism Formulae | 125

Appendix 2: Why most Jews do not consider claims for Jesus as Messiah | 127

Appendix 3: Some words that have changed meaning | 135

Appendix 4: Shabbat Dinner | 141

Appendix 5: Humanity | 145

Appendix 6: Dispensationalism | 147

Appendix 7: Unitarian History | 149

Bibliography | 152

Acknowledgments

I am indebted to myriad friends and mentors who have been my guides over the fifty-some years that I've been studying the Scriptures.

The Rev Jim McKendrick, former rector of Calvary Episcopal Church in Rockdale, Pennsylvania, who saw ministry potential in me and took me and a few other of his acolytes on a tour of his alma mater, Philadelphia Divinity School.

My professor in another seminary who showed me that I would never make it in a mainstream denomination by telling us in a lecture, "When you get out into your pulpits, don't you lie to your people and tell them that any of this is true." I didn't finish that program.

The friend who took me to a meeting of the off-brand, parachurch teaching ministry where I heard the Bible and logic in the same sentence for the first time.

Rabbi Mark Levin, spiritual leader (emeritus) of Congregation Beth Torah in Overland Park, Kansas, who helped me refine some important ideas.

Friends and coworkers who lent me books and introduced me to teachers and ministries I would not have otherwise found.

The folks at Wipf & Stock who patiently led me through the publication process.

Of course, my wife Karen who is incredibly supportive and patient.

Preface

If either of my parents were religiously observant, they would not have married each other. Dad was Jewish, Mom was Episcopalian. They set out to raise us kids as unaffiliated. In the 1950s, you could only raise children without a religious education if you lived more than fifty miles from Grandma. If Bubbe doesn't shlep the grandkids to Sunday school, Nana will.

It came to pass as the extended family was gathered at Nana-and-Gramps's house for a major dinner, it could have been Thanksgiving or merely some Sunday, that we kids were rounded up and ordered to entertain the adults by singing *Jesus Loves Me*. My sister and I were the only ones who didn't know the words.

This state of affairs gave Nana great concern. She started taking us to Sunday school at her Methodist church. According to family stories, Dad didn't mind us going. What bugged him was that his mother-in-law was butting in. He told Mom, "If you want them to go to church, then you find a church and we'll take them." She chose an Episcopal church. Thus began my religious education.

I loved the Eucharist. We were using the 1928 edition of the Book of Common Prayer, which still used Elizabethan English. In my naiveté, I thought that the old-fashioned language was inherently religious, and not merely old-fashioned. When I first saw Shakespeare's *Macbeth* performed on *Hallmark Hall of Fame* in the days of live, black-and-white TV, I wondered why the Bard wrote in religious language. And why were Lady Macbeth's ladies-in-waiting nuns? At least that's what they looked like to me.

Preface

I became an acolyte, as we called our altar boys. I could have recited the Communion service as well as the priest, from memory. It wouldn't have counted, of course, because only a properly ordained priest may perform a sacrament.

When the Episcopal Church began to revise the prayerbook in the late 1960s, it finally dawned on me, in a forehead slapping moment, that God hadn't written the previous edition. From this awakening of interest, began my search for understanding and Truth with a capital T.

The first thing I tried to understand was arguably the most important, since it is always at the top of anybody's list of Articles of Faith. I refer, of course, to the doctrine of Trinity. The kids at Young Life told me that I wasn't supposed to understand it; I was supposed to "take it on faith." If I don't understand what I'm supposed to believe, I asked, how do I know that I believe it correctly? This only irritated them.

I had had limited instruction in the Bible. We didn't do Bible stories in Sunday school, like the Baptists. There were the "Propers," the appointed lectionary readings from the Gospels and Epistles for each Sunday and holiday, and that was about it.

There was a ritual called the Christmas Pageant. This was a series of tableaux where young children in bathrobes posed while an adult read a script. Included in the script was the passage from Luke called the Annunciation. The Angel tells Mary, "The Holy Ghost shall come upon thee, and the power of the Highest shall overshadow thee: therefore, also that holy thing which shall be born of thee shall be called the Son of God." This fit with the creed we recited every week, wherein Jesus is said to be "incarnate by the Holy Ghost of the Virgin Mary . . . "

As I pondered these words in prayer, trying to understand what I was called upon to believe, I had what I call a "naked emperor moment:" If words have meaning, as I believe they do, then the Holy Ghost (whatever that means) *is* the Father. These are not two distinct "Persons," but two *titles* for the same individual. I cannot unsee that. I have never understood why so many others refuse to see it.

Preface

My search took me to several groups, denominations, organizations, whose names are pretty much irrelevant to the story. Providence led me to a heterodox parachurch teaching ministry. It was at my first gathering there that I first heard logic and Bible used in the same paragraph. Orthodox Christians typically told me that I couldn't compare my logic with God's. My reply was that I wasn't comparing my logic with God's; I was comparing my logic with theirs. They usually insisted that their internally inconsistent, contradictory, and equivocating arguments were logical, even if they could not understand them, themselves.

That meeting where I first heard the Bible presented logically was more than 50 years ago. Since then, my only question is "What does the Bible [actually] say?" and not what any creed, dogma, denomination, or sect requires. I only want to know what is true; I do not care what any articles of faith demand, or what doctrines a synod calls fundamental. Naturally, I have been shown the door more than once, typically after saying something to the effect of, "No, the Bible doesn't actually say that."

Accepting conventional wisdom, because it is conventional, is the essence of fundamentalism. The word *fundamentalist* does not refer to one who believes the Bible literally. Instead, it refers to one who believes a set of fundamental doctrines, simply because they are required, fundamental doctrines and not necessarily because the Bible voluntarily supports the view. (It may, in fact, support a particular doctrine, but a fundamentalist is one who believes the doctrine, because it is called fundamental without regard to what the Bible actually says.)

According to legend, when Martin Luther was on trial for heresy, he argued to the Court, "If I am wrong, convict me out of Scripture." The Judge answered, "That's what all the heretics say."

The term "fundamentalist" comes from a multi-volume commentary, published in about 1910 by BIOLA, the Bible Institute of Los Angeles, titled *The Fundamentals*. It has various authors. Each chapter describes a "fundamental" doctrine which, in the opinion of the authors, all Christians are required to believe in order to be properly called Christian. Since it is my position that the Bible

Preface

does not voluntarily support all of their fundamental doctrines, I suggest that the proper term for one who believes the Bible literally is not "fundamentalist," but "heretic."

The disciples in Berea "were more noble than those in Thessalonica, in that they received the word with all readiness of mind, and searched the scriptures daily, whether those things were so."[1] Paul advised the Thessalonians to "Prove all things; hold fast that which is good."[2] It is the duty of "ordinary" disciples to immerse themselves in Scripture and keep their leaders on the ball. We must test everything, including and especially the things we were taught are "fundamental."

When Apollos, a travelling preacher with an incomplete knowledge of the Gospel, came to Ephesus,[3] two believers, Aquila and Priscilla, took him aside and "expounded unto him the way of God more perfectly." It is tempting to rely on expert professionals, but as we shall see, history has shown that even in the sphere of eternal verities, pastors also need pastoring.

So, what follows is my current opinion, after a half-century of study. None of the ideas expressed is original to me. Everything I know, I have learned from somebody. My practice is to read just about anybody's literature; there may be an argument that I haven't seen before. I could be wrong in any of this. Please don't believe something merely because this little volume is published. Be a Berean: examine every word by the criterion of Scripture. And I mean by Scripture, not what somebody told you it really means when it says something else. Because what I have learned over these fifty years is that what is called Christianity is not merely a deviation from the first century Nazarean Judaism of Rabbi Yeshua bar Yosef ha-Notzri; the two are completely unrelated to each other. As Robin Meyer said in his Lyman Beecher Lectures at Yale, "The greatest illusion of all . . . is the idea that anything resembling early Christian discipleship would be recognized, or tolerated, in the present age."[4]

1. Acts 17:11.
2. 1 Thess 5:21.
3. Acts 18:24–26.
4. Meyers, *Spiritual*, 44.

Introduction

IN FIDDLER ON THE *Roof*, Tevye the dairyman delivers a folk saying from time to time attributing it to the Bible. "As the Good Book says," he tells his fellows, "When a poor man eats a chicken, one of them is sick." As it happens, that proverb appears nowhere in Scripture. Unfortunately for Tevye, he has so little time to study that he is unaware that the Good Book says no such thing. In like manner, Rabbinic sages spend their time studying the Talmud rather than "the Good Book" and assume that *halakhah*, Jewish Law, derives from the *Tanakh*, the Hebrew Bible.

Christians have similar sayings. They may recite, "You *are* a spirit, you *have* a soul, and you *live* in a body;" or "God exists eternally in three persons . . . " or "When you die, you step out of your body into eternity," as though these sayings were biblical. As we will see, none of these sayings can be found in Scripture, either. They are all products of Greek philosophy, mostly Platonist, with which the post-apostolic leaders replaced the Hebrew Bible as their source of authority.

As a result of relying on extra-biblical authority, neither mainstream Judaism nor mainstream Christianity is authentic to its founding. We could draw a straight line from Abraham, through Moses, King David, the Prophets and Jesus of Nazareth and we would find ourselves, not in Christianity nor Judaism, but in a no-man's-land somewhere between them.

Neither Yavne nor Antioch

It is common knowledge that Christianity grew out of Judaism. But Chilton and Neusner[1] quite reasonably ask the questions, "Which Christianity?" and "Which Judaism?" There was much diversity in what eventually became Christianity in late antiquity.[2] Even as the New Testament was being written, sects and divisions were forming. "[E]very one of you saith, I am of Paul; and I of Apollos; and I of Cephas; and I of Christ. Is Christ divided?"[3] This suggests that both unity and the Apostles' doctrine were lost very early.

Nor was Judaism at all monolithic. The main sects were the Pharisees, the Sadducees, the Essenes and the Zealots. Kristofer Carlson reports:

> Epiphanius of Salamis (c. 310–320 – 403 CE) describes twelve specific sects of the Jews: the Samaritans, the Essenes, the Sebuaeans, the Gorothenes, the Dositheans, the Sadducees, the Scribes, the Pharisees, the Hemerobaptists, the Nasaraeans, the Ossaeans, and the Herodians. The Jerusalem Talmud (c. 200 – 400 CE) quotes Rabbi Johanan as saying there were twenty-four heretical sects of Judaism in the time of Ezekiel.[4]

Each of these sects had its multiple schools of thought. Among the Pharisees, the two best known were the School of Hillel and the School of Shammai. Into this mix, came a reformer from Nazareth, who set about calling the "lost sheep of the House of Israel"[5] back to the Law of Moses from which they had strayed.

So, from which Judaism did Christianity spring? The unfortunate, but inescapable, conclusion is that what is today called mainstream, Nicene Christianity is entirely unrelated to first century "Nazarean" Judaism. Equally unfortunate and inescapable is the conclusion that present-day Rabbinic Judaism is not truly representative of the Torah delivered to us by *Moshe Rabbenu*, Moses

1. Chilton and Neusner, *Judaism*.
2. Ehrman, *Lost*, 1–3.
3. 1 Cor 1:12–13.
4. Carlson, *Development*, 10.
5. Matt 15:24.

Introduction

our Teacher. Just as there have always been, even to the present day, varieties of non-Nicene Christianity, so also there has always been, and continues to be non-Rabbinic Judaism.[6]

Nor is it easy to pigeon-hole the Rabbi from Nazareth. He has been called an Orthodox Jew and a reformer. Rabbi David Zaslow says that he is a *maggid*, a teacher who teaches through stories.[7] Seeing how Jesus' rulings on *halachah*, Jewish law, often line up with those of the great Pharisee sages, especially Rabbi Hillel, Rabbi Harvey Falk concludes that he was a Pharisee.[8] When Yeshua told his followers not to follow the *takkanot* and *ma'asim* of the Pharisees,[9] he looks like a Karaite. He famously said, "Ye have heard that it hath been said, Thou shalt love thy neighbour, and hate thine enemy, But I say unto you, Love your enemies, bless them that curse you, do good to them that hate you, and pray for them which despitefully use you, and persecute you,"[10] The phrase "hate your enemy" does not appear anywhere in the Hebrew Scriptures. It does, however, appear in the Qumran writings, leading some to conclude that he was an Essene.

Jesus of Nazareth cannot be fit neatly into any denominational category. We can confidently assert that he was definitely Jewish, being descended from King David from the Tribe of Judah. We can also confidently assert that he most definitely was not a Christian, as that word is understood today.

The movement that arose from Yeshua's ministry of "about a year"[11] has been called "Primitive Christianity," "Nazarean Judaism," the "Jesus Movement." None of these terms is entirely satisfactory. They all carry baggage of later, anachronistic, sectarian meanings. For lack of a more accurate, more neutral term, we will

6. Costa, *Remarks*, 92–118.
7. Zaslow, *Jesus*.
8. Falk, *Jesus*.
9. Matt 23:3.
10. Matt 5:43.
11. Rood, *Chronological*.

use Nazarean Judaism, as being perhaps the least unsatisfactory. We will seek that narrow path that few find.[12]

It is important to distinguish first century Nazarean Judaism from the modern Messianic Jewish movement. Messianic Judaism maintains Nicene articles of faith, as is standard in mainstream Christianity. It has been described as "Evangelical Christianity, with a thin veneer of *Yiddishkeit* (Ashkenazic Jewish culture)." Its creedal statements would put it squarely within Protestantism, except that their Sabbath observance on Saturday instead of Sunday and eating biblically make them "heretical" according to the Christian mainstream. They embrace post-Apostolic dogma while practicing rabbinic *takanot* and *ma'asim*, which Jesus told his disciples to avoid,[13] thereby living with the worst of both worlds. The modern movement was originally known as "Hebrew Christian," which I suggest is a more accurate description.

---

12. Cf. Matt 7:14.
13. Matt 23:3.

Methodology

My training is as a lawyer in the Anglo-American Common Law tradition. I bring the principles of legal interpretation I learned in Law School to interpreting the Sacred Text. As it happens, the methods used by common lawyers are essentially the same as the Rabbis use in interpreting *halachah*, Jewish law. This is because in the early days of formation of the English Common Law, there was significant Jewish influence in the royal court.[1]

This book is my brief. Briefs have two main functions. One is to advise the client objectively what the law is in the client's situation, following the evidence wherever it may lead,[2] without regard to what the client *wants* the law to be. The other is to advocate a particular position hoping to persuade a court to rule in favor of the lawyer's client. Of course, only a lawyer can write 200 pages and still call it a "brief."

---

1. Bacon and Gilbert, eds., *Atlas*, 69.

2. When the police investigate a crime, say a homicide, they first look for evidence to eliminate potential suspects. This is why they always look first at close family and friends of the victim. If investigators rush to judgment and only seek out evidence that supports their initial hunch, then defense counsel will rip their case apart at trial. Only by eliminating false leads and erroneous suspicions will the proper suspect be convicted beyond a reasonable doubt. Many times, biblical theorists will only examine the text in ways that support their pet theories. When the Scripture does not explicitly support a favorite doctrine, it will be claimed that the doctrine is the "best inference" from the explicit data. For that to be the case, all other possible inferences must be tested. This is rarely done.

My intent is the first purpose, to seek truth, not to advocate a position, but to discover God's Law. The reader is the client, in this analogy, not the judge. Before one can decide whether one believes what is written, one must discover what really *is* written. I have heard people say to the effect of, "I don't believe the Bible literally, because I don't believe [something that it doesn't actually say]." Those who have decided *a priori* not to believe what is written have less incentive to read carefully than those who do believe. Similarly, those who have chosen to accept fundamental doctrines, because they were taught that those doctrines were fundamental, are hindered in their ability to adjust their positions if challenged by the text.

I have little confidence that what I write here will change many minds. As Kuhn noted, people rarely change their opinion unless confronted with overwhelming evidence.[3] This is my effort to "be ready always to give an answer to every man that asketh you a reason of the hope that is in you with meekness and fear."[4] Whatever model people work from, they will continue using it as long as it continues to be useful. That a model works does not necessarily mean that the model is "true," only that it is useful. When a better model comes along, it will be adopted by newcomers to its field, but will become the standard only when the old guard still using the previous model die off or retire.

Fifty years before Copernicus published his heliocentric model of the universe, Christopher Columbus sailed to the New World using the then-current Ptolemaic geocentric model for astronomical navigation. To induce Jamaican locals to continue supplying provisions to his crew, he pretended to command an eclipse of the sun on February 29, 1504. He knew to expect an eclipse because ships carry an almanac of astronomical information. Astronomers using the Ptolemaic model had accurately predicted the eclipse.

The Ptolemaic model worked, and was therefore useful, but was cumbersome and complicated. Copernicus' model replaced

---

3. Kuhn, *Revolutions*.
4. I Pet 3:15.

Methodology

Ptolemy's model because it is more elegant and simple and therefore more useful. It is incidentally also more true.

The heliocentric model is counter-intuitive, contrary to ordinary people's observation and contradicts common misinterpretation of figurative biblical language as literal statements of fact. The geocentric model of the universe was also preserved by Vatican decrees. Galileo's work was on the Index of banned books from 1633 to 1992.[5] In the meantime, loyal church-related educational institutions, especially Jesuit ones, were bound to teach according to dogma.[6]

PRINCIPLES OF LEGAL INTERPRETATION INCLUDE:

Entirety within the "four corners" of the document:

If the language is clear and unambiguous, evidence from outside the document cannot change the meaning of what is written. Contracts usually have a clause to the effect of, "This contract is the entirety of the agreement; no other representations have been made by either party." Similarly, a criminal statute which does not spell out completely and exactly what behavior is prohibited does not give proper notice to someone who might be inclined to commit that behavior and is therefore "void for vagueness."

The Bible is the written contract between the Creator and His people. For our purposes, we assume the standard 66-book Protestant canon as a single document. Promises or requirements not contained within the four corners of the document are not canonical.

---

5. NewScientist, *Vatican*.
6. Stimson, *Acceptance*.

Non-contradiction:

It would be unworkable for a contract or a criminal statute to both require and forbid the same thing. A proper interpretation must resolve ambiguities or apparent contradictions.

For example, Jesus' crucifixion is described four times in the four Gospels. There are differences among the various accounts. In Luke chapter 23, Jesus and two other condemned prisoners are led to Calvary and crucified. Then, those watching mocked him, the soldiers divided his clothing among themselves. They set up his accusation. One of the other prisoners insulted him, but the other believed and was promised Paradise. In Matthew 27 and Mark 15, Jesus was led to Golgotha and crucified. The soldiers divided his clothes and set up the accusation. *Then* two other prisoners were brought and crucified. Both of them hurled insults. Finally, John is more concise. He was taken to Golgotha, "where they crucified him, and two others with him, on either side one, and Jesus in the midst." (19:18) As written, these do not seem to fit. But this is not hopeless.

The word "one" in the phrase "on either side one" does not appear in the Greek. It was added by the translators to make the translation align with tradition. John tells us that they crucified Jesus and two others on either side. That is literally, "two on this side and on that side" and Yeshua in the middle, for a total of five crucifees, a slow day for a Roman crucifixion detail.

Reading all four accounts in harmony, we see that Jesus and two other prisoners were led to Calvary/Golgotha and crucified. The soldiers divided his clothes, put up an accusation, etc., and *then* brought two more prisoners. This interpretation harmonizes the texts but challenges traditional teaching. Where tradition and text conflict, the text must prevail. Tradition comes from outside the "four corners."

Consistency of meaning:

A word or phrase must be consistent in its meaning throughout the document. Many contracts have a section early in the document for definitions. A preprinted form might refer to the parties as "Buyer" and "Seller." The definitions section will define early for the entire document who is who and what terms mean.

The Bible works similarly. The first time an expression is used, it will usually be defined. Volumes have been written speculating about the nature of Paul's "thorn in the flesh."[7] All manner of physical ailments have been suggested. The first time a similar phrase occurs is in Numbers 33:55: "But if ye will not drive out the inhabitants of the land from before you; then it shall come to pass, that those which ye let remain of them shall be pricks in your eyes, and thorns in your sides, and shall vex you in the land wherein ye dwell." Paul, being well versed in the Hebrew Scriptures, would be familiar with this passage. His thorn in the flesh then, is most likely vexatious people, "Satan's messenger," and not a disease.

Many Christians read the Bible as though it began with the Gospel of Matthew. In some circles it is taught that the "New" Testament is entirely new and unrelated to the "Old," or that the "New" supersedes the "Old." We assume herein that the entire 66-book canon is a single document. The two sections work together. They are not hostile to each other.

Plain meaning

In general, the plain, ordinary meaning of words should prevail. This is not necessarily the literal meaning, but usually will be. See Luke 13:34 and Matthew 23:37, where Jesus speaking for his Father says, "Jerusalem, Jerusalem, you who kill the prophets and stone those sent to you, how often I have longed to gather your children together, as a hen gathers her chicks under her wings,

---

7. 2 Cor 12:7. And lest I should be exalted above measure through the abundance of the revelations, there was given to me a thorn in the flesh, the messenger of Satan to buffet me.

and you were not willing." The Father is not literally a chicken. This is the figure of speech "simile." Or consider Mark 9:47, "And if thine eye offend thee, pluck it out: it is better for thee to enter into the kingdom of God with one eye, than having two eyes to be cast into hell fire." The plain meaning of this verse is an example of the figure of speech "hyperbole." A hyperbole is an exaggeration to illustrate how important the point being made is.[8]

Read what is written

This is included in the principle of plain meaning. I once heard a radio preacher claim that any person who does not confess that Jesus is God in the flesh is not of God, but of the Devil. To back up his claim, he cited 1 John 4:1–3:

> Beloved, believe not every spirit, but try the spirits whether they are of God: because many false prophets are gone out into the world. Hereby know ye the Spirit of God: Every spirit that confesseth that Jesus Christ is come in the flesh is of God: And every spirit that confesseth not that Jesus Christ is come in the flesh is not of God: and this is that *spirit* of antichrist, whereof ye have heard that it should come; and even now already is it in the world.

From even the most cursory reading of the text, it is clear that this passage does not say what the preacher said that it means. There is a significant difference between a "spirit" confessing and a "person" confessing something. There is an infinite difference between having "come" in the flesh and being "God" in the flesh. We must guard against the danger of reading what we expect to see, rather than what is truly there. Similarly, Laurence Brown argues that since Mohammed was a person who confessed that Jesus

---

8. Bullinger identifies over 200 different figures of speech. Most of us only learned a few in high school English classes: simile, metaphor, hyperbole, etc. Bullinger, *Figures*.

Methodology

Christ has come in the flesh, Mohammad was from God.⁹ Again, there is a significant difference between "spirit" and "person."¹⁰

I do not impute nefarious intent to either of these men. There are, however, unscrupulous charlatans who twist the Scriptures beyond recognition, while hoping that their audiences will not read their bibles any more carefully than these two.

Plain meaning includes technical terms or legal "terms of art" which have particular meanings. "Ounce" can mean different weights, depending on what is being weighed. Produce is measured in ounces *avoirdupois*; gold is weighed in Troy ounces. A Troy pound of silver weighs less than a pound of rice. The word "exchange" in "legalese" means a "barter or swap" and excludes payment in cash. I once represented a defendant charged with prostitution. The statute under which she was charged prohibited performing or agreeing to perform certain activities for hire, "where there is an exchange of value." The Legislature had written this statute badly. They should have said "for consideration," rather than "exchange." "Consideration" is a legalese term for whatever payment is made for a promise, whether money, goods, or another promise. I argued that the defendant could not have met all the elements of the offense, because the undercover cop paid her in cash, which is excluded from the definition of "exchange."

---

9. Brown, *Misgod'ed*, 181. It is outside my competence to opine on what form or forms of Islam are authentic to Mohammed. Brown refers to Sunni as "Orthodox" Islam.

10. See also Matt 24:4-5. When asked about signs of the end and his second advent, Yeshua answers, "Take heed that no man deceive you. For many shall come in my name, saying, I am Christ; and shall deceive many." This was written before the invention of punctuation. It could as easily be rendered that the future deceivers would "confess" that Yeshua is the Messiah as punctuated, or to quote them as claiming to be the Messiah, themselves. In either event, people who seem to say all the right things could still be deceiving and themselves deceived. The Hebrew or Aramaic of the day did not have a form of indirect quotation.

Avoiding absurd conclusions

The judge did not buy my argument, in part because the "plain meaning" rule also includes avoiding absurd conclusions. John Locke, in his 1695 classic, *The Reasonableness of Christianity*,[11] reminds us that biblical religion is perfectly reasonable, though many "systems of divinity" are not. Theologians would do well to observe this principle. Apparently, the Church Father Tertullian never really said, "*Credo quia absurdum est*," "I believe it because it is absurd," but many seem to follow the dictum anyway.

Words mean what they meant when they were written

In *Romeo and Juliet*, Shakespeare has the two lovers on Juliet's balcony, pledging their undying love for each other, when Juliet's nurse calls to her to come inside and go to bed. Juliet yells back to her "By and by, I come." When the Bard was writing 400-plus years ago, "by and by" meant "immediately." She is saying "I'm coming, right away." Its meaning has changed over the centuries to "sometime in the future," as in the hymn "In the Sweet By-and-by."

When Yeshua was asked about the end times, he describes some signs, and adds "But the end *is* not by and by."[12] That is, the end is not "immediate." A modern reader might think that the end is not to be expected eventually, by and by, sometime in the future, but will happen immediately on the appearance of these signs.[13]

The cultural context of the writing is an indispensable consideration. When we remember that the entire Scripture was written to a thoroughly Hebrew audience, we can read it with a Hebrew lens. If we read Hebraic thoughts through a Hellenistic lens, we will not understand the original intent of the author.

To really understand what the words in the New Testament meant to their original audience, we must transport ourselves in

---

11. Locke, *Reasonableness*, 5.
12. Luke 21:7–9.
13. For a discussion of some words which now have different meanings from their biblical usage, see Appendix 3, below.

Methodology

our imagination to first century, Roman-occupied Galilee and Judea. We need to remove ourselves from modernity.

We moderns, or post moderns, living in the twenty-first century think about the world as we see it. We tend to think that our thought patterns, the kinds of questions we ask, the incentives that motivate us, are the same thoughts, questions, and motivations that all humans have had throughout time and across cultures.[14]

Just as becoming fluent in a new language requires thinking in the new language, and not translating back and forth to and from our mother tongue, we need to learn to think like a late second temple era, Hebrew-speaking Judean or Galilean. Most of us have a limited vocabulary, and we speak Bible with a western, materialist accent.

There is a growing body of evidence that the New Testament, especially the Gospels[15] and Acts, was originally written in Hebrew. Scholars such as Nehemia Gordon[16] and Miles Jones[17] are finding and publishing previously unknown copies of the manuscripts of the New Testament, especially the Gospels, which the first generation of disciples carried to far off mission fields. Jones writes that the Hebrew textual tradition survived and fueled, in part, the Protestant Reformation.

Douglas Hamp[18] makes a compelling case that Yeshua taught primarily in the Hebrew Language, and that Hebrew, not Aramaic,

---

14. Cadbury, *Modernization*.

15. Both Gordon and Jones mention the use of paronomasia in Hebrew writing. They both also bring the example of the Annunciation, where the Angel tells Joseph that Mary "shall bring forth a son, and thou shalt call his name JESUS: for he shall save his people from their sins." Mt 1:21. The paronomasia makes sense only in Hebrew. "You will call his name *Yeshua*, because *yisha* (he will save) his people from their sins." In Greek, it reads "You will call him *Iesous*, because *sozei* (he will save) his people. The Peshita Aramaic reads, "You will call his name *Yeshua*. because [nun-chet-yud-vav-heh-yud]. Without vowel points, I can speculate a pronunciation for he-will-save along the lines of NeChYUHai. Suffice it to say that the paronomasia does not appear in Greek nor Aramaic, but Hebrew alone.

16. Gordon, *Yeshua*.

17. Jones, *Sons*.

18. Hamp, *Discovering*.

was the national language of *Eretz Yisrael* at the time. Those words commonly identified as Aramaic in the New Testament, he shows are either common to both Hebrew and Aramaic or are exclusively Hebrew. Until the discovery of the Dead Sea Scrolls, scholars generally assumed that Hebrew had gone extinct, except for liturgical uses. The Scrolls demonstrate that Hebrew was a living language still. Any teacher who wishes to communicate to his audience would not likely use a dead language foreign to their ears.

It is an article of faith in mainstream textual criticism that the New Testament was written in Greek, and that the Gospels were not likely reduced to writing until the second century. There is a minority view that Aramaic was the original language. If this is correct, then the Aramaic versions would likely predate the Greek.[19] Both Greek and Aramaic primacists assume that Hebrew was no longer a living language in first century Judea. The Dead Sea scrolls contain original works of the Qumran community written in Hebrew, demonstrating that Hebrew was still very much alive.

If the Hebrew versions are in fact original, then the dates of first writing can be pushed back as far as immediately after the reported incidents occurred. Early dating of the original monographs would allow for the various books to have been written by the authors to whom they are traditionally attributed. The eyewitness reports would then be genuine eyewitness testimony. As John says in his first epistle, "That which we have seen and heard declare we unto you . . . ."[20]

Even if New Testament writers wrote in Greek, they still had a Hebraic mindset. Where we read the word "hell" in the Nazarean Writings (the New Testament), it is commonly translated from the Greek word "*hades*." Rather than looking to Homeric literature to see how *hades* is used, we will look to the Septuagint to see that *hades* is the closest available Greek word to the Hebrew *sheol*. *Hades* and *sheol* are not quite synonymous. They both refer to the state of the dead. To the Greeks, the disembodied immortal souls of the

---

19. Except that the Peshita seems to be an Aramaic translation of the Greek, since it uses some Greek words transliterated with Aramaic characters.

20. 1 John 1:3.

Methodology

dead were thought to be alive and conscious in the underworld known as *Hades*; to the Hebrews, *Sheol* is the "grave"[21] where the dead sleep until the resurrection at the end of days.

Scripture interprets Scripture

This is a reiteration of the principles of reading what is written within the four corners. The immediate context and the overall scope will give us what we need to know. Many unbiblical doctrines have been falsely supported by taking a verse, or part of a verse out of context. The Bible says, " . . . There is no God.[22]" The full sentence is "The fool hath said in his heart, 'There is no God.'" As many modern preachers have said, "when you take the text out of the context, all you have left is the 'con.'"

As mentioned above, we will assume the standard, American Protestant 66-book canon. Carlson[23] mentions nine different sets of New Testament Scriptures considered canonical by various churches. We use the Protestant canon as the one most widely accepted among this book's likely readers. As any attorney can tell you, evidence is not proof. Proof is whatever persuades the "trier of fact," the jury. Evidence which the jury will not accept wastes the jury's time and may well dissuade rather than persuade them.

Most quotations from Scripture will be from the King James Version. There are several reasons for this, including: a) it is in public domain, so there is no need to get permission to quote from it; b) the standard reference works such as Strong's Exhaustive Concordance and Young's Analytical Concordance are keyed to the KJV; and c) the archaic language distinguishes between singular and plural in the second grammatical person, between "thou" and "ye," as most languages other than modern English, including the biblical languages, still do. Also, d) the KJV distinguishes LORD from Lord. When the original has the Name, *Yud He Vav He*,

---

21. "Gravedom" might be a better rendering, to distinguish the state from *qeber* which is the physical tomb or hole in the ground.

22. Ps 14:1.

23. Carlson, *Development*, 3.

YHVH or Yehovah, we see L̲ord in small caps; when the original has a form of *Adon* or *Kyrios*, we see Lord in upper and lower case. The distinction is important, as we will see.

Misunderstood Teachings

MANY OF YESHUA'S TEACHINGS are misunderstood, due to failure of the reader to read them in the context of Roman-occupied Israel. We will look at three particular teachings which contemporary Americans commonly read as instructing Christians to be "doormats for Jesus."

> Whosoever shall smite thee on thy right cheek, turn to him the other also. And if any man will sue thee at the law, and take away thy coat, let him have thy cloke also. And whosoever shall compel thee to go a mile, go with him twain.[1]

These are not "nice things to do," or a command to masochistically take a beating. They are examples of aggressive non-violence. Non-violence is not "passive resistance;" there is nothing passive about it. The following analysis is adapted from *Engaging the Powers*, by Walter Wink. [2]

The three sayings are from the Sermon on the Mount. The target demographic for that discourse was the marginalized, the poor, and downtrodden. The Beatitudes, "blessed are the poor in spirit," "blessed are those who hunger and thirst after righteousness," gave hope to the hopeless.

Who, in that day, could "smite thee on the cheek" with impunity? Any Roman. Who could "compel thee to go a mile?" Again,

---

1. Matt 5:39–41.
2. Wink, *Engaging*.

any Roman. Who would sue a destitute debtor for his only clothes? Probably a Roman.

How could an oppressed Hebrew regain some honor and control over his life? Through aggressive non-violence.

A "smite" on the right cheek would probably be a backhand slap. Its purpose would not be to do physical injury. It would be to put an uppity Judean in his place. To the one smitten, the damage would be to his pride and to his public sense of honor. The natural impulse would be to strike back. In that event, if the Roman is armed, he could legally simply kill the upstart where he stood. This would not be the desired outcome for the one insulted.

Instead, Yeshua suggests offering the left cheek as a target. In so doing the one insulted refuses to accept the shame imposed and claims parity with the oppressor. If the Roman were to strike the left cheek, without provocation, it would be a punch with his right hand (his shield would be on his left arm) and would be a battery giving rise to the right of self-defense. Turning the other cheek is not simply standing there, taking a beating.

Any Roman soldier had the power to impress into service a civilian and compel him to carry the soldier's pack. There was a one-mile limit. The Romans were not stupid; they knew that even oppressed peoples would only tolerate so much. After a mile, the civilian was to be released. The soldier could then grab the next civilian he saw and press him into service.

If he compelled or allowed anyone to carry his pack more than one mile, he could be subject to discipline, at his centurion's discretion. The civilian insisting on going the extra mile is reclaiming control of his life and potentially causing the soldier a lot of trouble. To be sure, the second mile would be no more enjoyable than the first. But the civilian regains some control and dignity.

We see this in operation when Yeshua was so badly beaten that he could no longer carry his cross, "they laid hold upon one Simon, a Cyrenian, coming out of the country, and on him they laid the cross, that he might bear it after Jesus."[3] Simon was in the

---

3. Luke 23:26. See also Matt 27:32 and Mark 15:21.

wrong place at the wrong time and was summarily pressed into service. How far he actually carried the cross is not recorded.

"[I]f any man will sue thee at the law, and take away thy coat, let him have thy cloke also." This brings up odd imagery. "Coat" in the Greek text *chiton* which is a loan word from Semitic origin from *kitenet*. They both mean a tunic, usually of cotton, worn next to the skin. "Cloke" is rendered from the Greek *himation*, which is a generic term for a garment, usually outerwear. The verse can be read, "If someone sues you for your skivvies, give him your overalls, too."

Anyone being sued for his skivvies is probably so poor that the clothes he is wearing are his only remaining possessions. There would be nothing else for the creditor to take. As today, a plaintiff would not bring a suit unless he expects both to win and to collect on the judgment. This poor defendant owes the debt. Again, this is not a blanket command to roll over and play dead for any frivolous lawsuit. This is a way for an oppressed defendant to shift shame from himself to the oppressor.

Torah requires that if a creditor takes a garment as collateral, he must return it by nightfall, since the debtor has no other blanket to sleep in.[4] It is a shameful thing to deprive the poor in this way. As the defendant is walking home from the courthouse naked, he will likely attract attention. When he explains his situation, the creditor's name will be tarnished in polite society.

St Francis of Assisi[5] was the son of Pietro Bernardone, a wealthy merchant. His father wanted him to follow him in the family business. Francis preferred the contemplative life. When Pietro threatened to cut Francis off from his trust fund, Francis stripped off his finery and said from now on, only God is my father. He then walked off naked and founded the Franciscan Order.

The ancients were not as frightened by nudity as 21st century Americans. They saw it as a sign of poverty, not lunacy, and poverty was seen as a symptom of God's disfavor. Peter famously

---

4. Exod 22:26.
5. Cunningham, *Nudity,* 357.

fished naked.⁶ The leading lady in Song of Songs recounts, " . . . I *am* black because the sun hath looked upon me." Cunningham writes that laborers in antiquity who had only one set of clothes to their name would commonly lay their clothes aside while working in the fields.⁷ Since second Temple times to the present, the ritual bath for purification in the *mikvah* is still done naked, according to *halachah*. Isaiah went "naked and barefoot" for three years at Yehovah's command.⁸

That Yeshua did not teach passive martyrdom is made clear in one of the last teaching sessions before his crucifixion:

> And he said unto them, When I sent you without purse, and scrip, and shoes, lacked ye any thing? And they said, Nothing. Then said he unto them, But now, he that hath a purse, let him take it, and likewise his scrip: and he that hath no sword, let him sell his garment, and buy one . . . And they said, Lord, behold, here are two swords. And he said unto them, It is enough.⁹

Clearly, the disciples were instructed to be neither "doormats for Jesus," nor a guerrilla force, since two swords among the twelve were sufficient.

---

6. John 21:7.
7. Cunningham, *Nudity*, 84.
8. Isa 20:3.
9. Luke 22:35–38.

Human History

WE HUMANS HAVE a less than stellar record when it comes to obedience to our Creator's instructions. In the Garden of Eden, we had only one rule: Don't eat the fruit from the tree of knowledge of good and evil. We managed to mess that up in short order. The Bible does not tell us explicitly how long it took our first ancestors to commit sin. The most likely estimates that I have heard range from six to 48 hours.

God had written His plan of redemption in the stars.[1] He gave the stars their names.[2] The names of the stars and constellations tend to remain fairly constant throughout history, though names might be translated from language to language. For example, Virgo in English is the Virgin; in Hebrew, it is called *Bethulah*, which also means Virgin. The Zodiacal year starts with Virgo and ends with Leo, the Lion of the Tribe of Judah.

Since people lived so much longer in those days before the Flood, there was plenty of time for a grandfather to teach several generations of descendants. There was no written text to pass down since the Torah was written in the stars. Astronomy is the law, science, instruction, *Torah* governing the movements of the heavenly bodies.

It was not long before we humans mucked things up so badly, that the Creator's only option was to wipe the slate clean and start over. There was one man, Noah, who was "perfect in his

---

1. Bullinger, *Witness*.
2. Ps 147:4.

generations, and [who] walked with God"[3] With about 120 years notice, God had Noah build a huge boat, rather like a barge, and collect animals so that there would be survivors of a great flood which was coming.

Once off the boat, God instructed humanity to be fruitful and multiply and fill the earth.[4] Naturally, instead of doing what we were told and filling the earth, we built a city and gathered in one place. God had to confuse our languages to get us to move and spread out.[5]

People forgot about the Creator and fell into polytheism. There was one man, Abram, who was faithful to God, so God counted his faithfulness as righteousness.[6] God told Abram to leave Ur, where he was living, and go to a "land I will show you."[7] Abram needed to get away from the corrupting influence of the city and out into the countryside where he could get acquainted with Yehovah, his Covenant Friend.

Once he had "crossed over" (Hebrew: *ever*) the Euphrates River with his wife and household, he became the first Hebrew (*evri*). Abram's descendants were known as Hebrews through their sojourn in Egypt. They had gone to Egypt because of a famine in Canaan, where they camped and tended their flocks.

There was a dynastic change in Egypt, and the Hebrews lost their favored status. They had had significant pull with the previous dynasty. Things got so bad that the Hebrews cried out to God for deliverance. In the manner of totalitarian tyrants throughout history, the Pharaoh was not inclined to release so many slaves all at once. God sent Moses with power to work miracles to convince the king to release the Hebrews. By Moses, God promised that there would come, sometime in the future, another prophet, from

---

3. Gen 6:9.
4. Gen 9:7.
5. Gen 11.
6. Rom 4:3, Jas 3:23, Gen 15:6.
7. Gen 12:1–3.

among his brethren, who would be like Moses. This prophet will speak only what God tells him; him we must hear and obey.[8]

The Hebrews were not the only ones who left. Exodus reports that they were a "mixed multitude"[9] After the refugees left Egypt, passing through the *Yam Suf* or *Yam Sof*, variously translated Red Sea, Sea of Reeds or End Sea, the People came to be known as *B'nei Yisrael*, the Children (or Descendants) of Israel.

Almost immediately, the people reverted to idolatry, making a calf idol modeled after the gods of Egypt. This was not pleasing to Yehovah. After a chastisement, the survivors were given a set of instructions, the *Torah*. *Torah*, in fact means "instruction" more than it means "law." Part of the instruction had to do with sacrifices, a sort of sacred barbeque. The Creator's instruction covers every aspect of life; it is instructions given for our good.[10]

The People of Israel arrive finally in the Promised Land and in short order, go astray again, this time after the gods of the Canaanites. At first glance, Canaanite fertility rituals look like a lot more fun than a barbecue. There is a dangerous spiral in the process of leaving Torah for the sexual impropriety of Baal worship.[11] It led the Israelites so far astray that they worshipped idols and sacrificed even their own children to Baal.

Yehovah sent a series of prophets to call the people back to Torah. Prophets are not usually popular people. Their main mission is to tell God's people what they are doing wrong, and what they need to do to get back to living rightly. This is not what people usually want to hear. Sometimes, the prophet feels so alone that he thinks he is the only one left among the faithful.[12] But the Creator

---

8. Deut 18:15.

9. Exod 12:38.

10. Deut 10:12–13.

11. Polytheistic theology in the ancient world held that gods and goddesses mating was the cause of the Earth's fertility. What inspired the gods and goddesses to mate was watching men and women mating. Orgies in antiquity were not merely wild parties, they were religious services praying for good crops.

12. e.g., Elijah, I Kgs 19:10.

always has a remnant, even when things look bleak, and it seems that all is lost.

As Paul Harvey used to say, "Self-government without self-discipline can't work." The people asked God for a king to rule over them, so they could be like the other nations.[13] God made this concession. He has made concessions to our human frailties from time to time. It was not His first choice, for example, to give us a law of divorce.[14]

The Kings did not make a good show of it, either. Solomon, the third king of a united Israel started off with a reputation as the wisest of men but ended up ruining the kingdom with excessive public works and building pagan shrines for his foreign wives. After his reign, the kingdom was divided into two. The Northern Kingdom kept the name Israel, the Southern Kingdom came to be known as Judah, after the tribe who supplied her kings.

The Northern Kingdom had zero good kings; the Southern had maybe two.

Israel went astray and rebelled against Yehovah and were exiled, scattered to the far reaches of the earth, where they remain to this day. Judah strayed later and was also exiled. Judah eventually repented and returned to the land of Israel, though many chose to remain in Babylonia. At this point, the remaining covenant people came to be known as Jews, from *Yehudim*, Judahites.

Once back in Judea, the remnant proved not to be highly skilled in self-government. Without a common enemy to unite them, faction turned against faction. In the power vacuum, Judea was conquered by the Greeks under Alexander. One of his successors, Antiochus Epiphanes, so offended the Judeans that they revolted. In the chaos following Syrian Greek rule, Judea was low-hanging fruit for the Romans to come and pick.

Early in the first century CE, at the height of Roman occupation, there arose a pair of reformers, cousins. They were known as Yochanan bar Zachariah ha-Kohen and Rabbi Yeshua bar Yosef.

---

13. 1 Sam 8:4–22.
14. Mark 10:1–9.

Human History

In English, their names are usually rendered John the Baptist and Jesus Christ.

The Cousins

YOCHANAN, CALLED THE IMMERSER, gathered a significant following. He dipped people in the Jordan River in a ceremony of repentance.[1] His crowds were large enough to make the civil authorities nervous. Anywhere in the Roman Empire where crowds gathered, especially in Judea, the bureaucrats and functionaries would presume that the assembly was plotting sedition. It was a reasonable presumption, especially in Judea.

The *Pax Romana*, Roman Peace, was maintained by keeping a tight lid on subjugated peoples. Subjugated peoples tend to resent being oppressed. But on the plus side, Roman forces maintained stability, which is necessary for commerce which, in turn, is necessary for raising tax revenues. In twentieth-century terms, we could say that Rome "made the trains run on time."[2]

Yochanan's cousin Yeshua came to be immersed. Yochanan identified his cousin as the "Lamb of God."[3] After his immersion, Yeshua went on a forty-day fasting retreat and then began his mission. Yochanan's mission was completed. Many of his followers

---

1. Matt 3:1–11.

2. In the middle of the twentieth century, the subject peoples of National Socialist and Fascist dictators excused their totalitarian repression saying, "At least he made the trains run on time." This may be urban legend, but the sentiment expressed is historically accurate.

3. John 1:29, 36.

migrated to Yeshua's ministry, as Yochanan had said "He must increase, but I *must* decrease."[4]

Yeshua's message was the same as Yochanan's, "Repent, for the kingdom of heaven is at hand."[5] He set about calling the "lost sheep of the House of Israel"[6] back to the Law of Moses from which they had strayed.

4. John 3:30.
5. Matt 4:17.
6. Matt 15:24.

Lost Sheep

THERE ARE MANY WAYS that sheep can get lost. There are those who assimilated into the prevailing Greco-Roman culture, and ate forbidden things, or committed labor on the Sabbath. Perhaps less obviously lost are those who follow man-made rules which purport to change what is written in the Torah, who "make the Word of God of no effect by their [religious] traditions."[1] These are people who believe that they are on the right path. It is more difficult for them to repent than it is for those who know that they have strayed.

When Isaiah warns of "woe to those who call good evil and evil good,"[2] we need to remember that when they do, they believe that the evil they do is good. Nobody wakes up in the morning saying, "Bwahaha, what evil can I do today and call it good?" The evil done in this world is committed by people who think that they are doing good, but with an erroneous opinion of what good is. People who know that they are doing wrong, thieves and telephone scammers, know that there is a limit to what they can get away with. There is no end to the evil potential of people who think that their evil is good. Yeshua predicted, "the time cometh, that whosoever killeth you will think that he doeth God service."[3]

Deliberately not taking sides here, we can say that this principle describes the divide between Democrats and Republicans in

1. Matt 15:1–6.
2. Isa 5:20.
3. John 16:2.

21st century America. Each party genuinely believes that its policies are "good," and the other party's policies are "evil." Sincerity is no guarantee of truth; they cannot both be right. The reality is that there will never be a political solution to a spiritual problem; looking to government for salvation is idolatry. And, no, the "other" party does not know that it is "wrong."

Rabbinic Judaism has a tradition that when God revealed the Torah to Moses on Mount Sinai, He revealed it in two forms. There is the Written Torah, which Moses was instructed to record in a scroll, and the Oral Torah, which was intended to be passed from generation to generation orally. For centuries, the Rabbis prohibited writing the Oral Torah, lest the people think that rabbinic writings were an additional Scripture.

As it happens their concern was well founded. Once the Talmud was compiled, it did not take long for it to supplant the *Tanakh* as the final authority for biblical interpretation.

Pirkei Avot, from the *Mishna*, tells us:

> Moses received the Torah from Sinai and transmitted it to Joshua; Joshua [transmitted it] to the Elders; the Elders [transmitted it] to the Prophets; and the Prophets transmitted it to the Men of the Great Assembly. They said three things: Be deliberate in judgment; develop many disciples; and make a fence for the Torah. [4]

According to the Rabbis, "Torah" in this passage refers to both the written Torah, the Five Books, and to the "Oral Torah." The Oral Torah is the instructions said to have been given to Moses to explain the details of how to keep the commandments of the Written Torah.

There is a story in the Talmud:

> On that day R. Eliezer brought forward every imaginable argument, but they did not accept them. Said he to them: "If the halachah agrees with me, let this carob-tree prove it!" Thereupon the carob-tree was torn a hundred cubits out of its place — others affirm, four hundred cubits. "No proof can be brought from a carob-tree," they retorted.

---

4. Davis, *Perkei*, 30.

Again he said to them: "If the halachah agrees with me, let the stream of water prove it!" Whereupon the stream of water flowed backwards — "No proof can be brought from a stream of water," they rejoined. Again he urged: "If the halachah agrees with me, let the walls of the schoolhouse prove it," whereupon the walls inclined to fall. But R. Joshua rebuked them, saying: "When scholars are engaged in a halachic dispute, what have ye to interfere?" Hence they did not fall, in honour of R. Joshua, nor did they resume the upright, in honour of R. Eliezer; and they are still standing thus inclined. Again he said to them: "If the halachah agrees with me, let it be proved from Heaven!" Whereupon a Heavenly Voice cried out: "Why do ye dispute with R. Eliezer, seeing that in all matters the halachah agrees with him!" But R. Joshua arose and exclaimed: "It is not in heaven." What did he mean by this? — Said R. Jeremiah: That the Torah had already been given at Mount Sinai; we pay no attention to a Heavenly Voice, because Thou hast long since written in the Torah at Mount Sinai, After the majority must one incline. R. Nathan met Elijah and asked him: What did the Holy One, Blessed be He, do in that hour? — He laughed [with joy], he replied, saying, "My sons have defeated Me, My sons have defeated Me."[5]

The Rabbis claim that when the Torah was transmitted through proper channels from Moses, eventually reaching them, that with the Torah came the authority to legislate new enactments and ordinances which add to and take away from the Written Torah. This story is used to support the notion that when God committed the Torah to the Sages, He no longer had any business messing with it. Torah no longer belongs to the Creator.

Rabbinic decrees are considered as on the same level with Scripture. It is claimed that the verse, "You are to act according to the word that they tell you from that place that God will have chosen; and you are to be careful to fulfill exactly as they instruct you" (Deut 17:11)[6] applies to rulings of the Rabbis.

5. Zahavy, *Talmud*.
6. Shurpin, *Why*.

Lost Sheep

The context of that verse is "matters of controversy" between two or more litigants. The judgment of the "judge that shall be in those days" is binding on those litigants, only. There is no mention of "rabbinic rulings," as this Torah was written by Moses more than a thousand years before the Rabbis came to be. When asked about the origin of an extra-biblical rabbinic enactment, the Rabbis will say that it came "from Moses on Sinai," that when Moses received the Torah from the hand of God on the mountain, he also received the entire Oral Law.

Once a ruling is accepted as Jewish Law, it is deemed to be part of the Oral Law, *halachah l'Moshe mi Sinai*, Law to Moses from [Mount] Sinai. Retroactive antiquity is imputed to rabbinic rulings. Christians fall victim to a similar fallacy. It is not uncommon for an orthodox Christian to claim that "All true Believers have always believed in the Trinity." Historically, this is nonsense.[7] The doctrine of Trinity took over 350 years to develop.

The early Pharisees taught what they called "the Tradition of the Elders."[8] They challenged Yeshua asking, "Why do your disciples transgress the tradition of the elders by not washing their hands when they eat bread?" He replied, "Why do you transgress the commandment of God by your traditions?"[9]

Moses tells us that no one has the authority to add to God's commandments, nor to diminish from them.[10] John of Patmos warns that to anyone who adds to the Book of the Revelation, God will add the plagues of the Apocalypse, and anyone who deletes anything from his Book will be deleted from the Book of Life.[11] Proverbs warns, "Add thou not unto his words, lest he reprove thee, and thou be found a liar."[12] Yeshua warns us that anyone who violates any of the Commandments of the Torah, and teaches

---

7. See Appendix 7 for a brief history of Unitarianism.
8. Matt 15:2; Mark 7:3, 5.
9. Matt 15:2–3.
10. Deut 4:2.
11. Rev 22:18–19.
12. Prov 30:6.

others to do the same will be called least in the Kingdom of God.[13] He may still perhaps enter the Kingdom, but not in high status.

Despite these warnings against the dangers of tampering with the Word of God, both the Bishops of the official Government "Church" and the Rabbis have arrogated to themselves the authority to alter and amend, add and subtract requirements of Scripture.

With the Torah, it is claimed that the authority to legislate was also transmitted. "Making a fence around the Torah" suggests legislative authority to set practical rules with some leeway between the rabbinic rules and the Torah, as a safeguard against inadvertently transgressing Torah. There is a natural tendency to think of the "fence" as the commandment, and then make another fence to safeguard against transgressing the first fence.

To be fair, there is normally a good reason for the *halachah*. When the Temple was destroyed, *circa* 70CE, there was no longer an active priesthood to receive testimony of the observation of the new moon, or of the "*aviv*"[14] state of the barley harvest. Thereafter the Sanhedrin took over the task of declaring the new moon or the new year. Just before the Sanhedrin was finally disbanded in the middle of the fourth century, they replaced the calendar based on eye-witness observation with a calculated calendar. The calculated calendar is still in use to this day. It is usually no more than one or two days off from what the date would be on the observed calendar.

Now, that observation can be made with great precision, and can be transmitted throughout the diaspora instantly, it is possible to return to the biblical calendar based on observation. However, since there is no recognized rabbinic court "greater in wisdom and number" than the defunct Sanhedrin, there is no body with the recognized authority to decree a return to the biblical calendar.

Another common practice among traditional Jews is never to pronounce the divine Name, YHVH or Yehovah, substituting

---

13. Matt 5:19.

14. Gordon, *Aviv*. If the barley crop has reached the "aviv" state of ripeness in the twelfth lunar month, then the next new moon will be the first month of the new year. If it has not, there will be a leap month added to the year.

Ha-Shem (the Name) Adonai, Adoshem, or some other circumlocution. The authorities are divided as to whether this custom came from Greek or Roman domination. The foreign rulers, attempting to bring uncooperative Judeans into line with the prevailing religious polytheism, prohibited keeping Sabbath, practicing circumcision and even speaking the name of Israel's God. The Sanhedrin decided, as a temporary measure until Messiah comes, to exercise the better part of valor and prohibit speaking God's actual name as it is spelled. Again, since there is no recognized Sanhedrin, there is no person or committee with the authority to lift the prohibition.

The Pharisees accused Yeshua of being a sinner and lawbreaker, in part because he went out of his way to violate their non-biblical rabbinic rules. Indeed, a common theme in many (some say all) stories of Yeshua's miracles is a specific challenge to the Pharisees' authority to legislate *halachah* which differs from the written Torah delivered to us from God by Moses.

We will see below how the custom of a particularly respected rabbi can turn into a "law" for his disciples, as when Rebbe Yochanan made a *halachah* about tying one's shoes. Or, when there is a question of where, exactly the line between Torah and sin is, the principle of making a fence around the Torah will lead to an unnecessarily restrictive ruling, just in case.

In *How to Run a Traditional Jewish Household*, Blu Greenberg writes:

> The Bible requires a minimum of seven days of [sexual] abstinence, beginning with the onset of [menstrual] flow and concluded by purification in the mikvah. The Rabbis expanded the minimum from seven days to twelve days – five-day minimum for the flow and seven "white" days following the last day of the flow.[15]

Biblically, seven days are required for a normal monthly flow,[16] and seven "white" days only after an unusual flow.[17] But the

---

15. Greenberg, *How*, 122–24.
16. Lev 15:19, 18:19, 20:18.
17. Lev 15:25–29.

Rabbis added the "white" days to the monthly regular cycle, adding more restriction to the commandment, just in case someone might mistake an unusual flow for a regular flow and inadvertently sin. A side effect of this restriction is that when the couple is allowed to resume relations, the wife will be at the part of her cycle where she is most fertile. Orthodox Jewish families tend to have many children.

The Nazareans

THAT THE EARLIEST FOLLOWERS of Yeshua were Jews is beyond controversy. To call them Jewish Christians, however, is anachronistic. Believers were first called Christians at Antioch,[1] *circa* 43CE.[2] In the New Testament, the term Christian is used exclusively to refer to Gentile converts who joined the Nazarean movement within Judaism. One could not call them Nazarean Jews, simply because they were not Jewish, unless they had undergone a rabbinically recognized conversion. Once a label was needed, it was a short step to call the followers of the *Christos* Christians.

The importance of the Jewishness of the early Nazarean movement cannot be overstated. An understanding of first century Jewish culture and of the Hebraic style of thinking is utterly indispensable to an understanding of the thoroughly Jewish New Testament writings. The New Testament cannot be comprehended without a solid foundation in the Old. Even the terms "old" an "new" are an unfortunate choice; "old" sounds outdated. Rabbi Zalman Schachter-Shalomi, the founder of Jewish Renewal, a fairly recent development in Rabbinic Judaism, suggests "elder" and "younger" testaments, to preserve the honor due to the *Tanakh*, the Hebrew Scriptures.[3]

---

1. Acts 11:26.
2. Bullinger, *Companion Bible*, appendix 180.
3. Zaslow, *Jesus*, introduction.

Yeshua used Hebraic vocabulary and concepts which are generally unknown to Gentile Christians.[4] Without Hebraic understanding, Christian readers miss the significance of the woman who was healed by touching Yeshua's *tzitzit*, fringes, on the corners of his garment. [5] They are unlikely to understand that when John was asked, "are you that prophet?"[6] the people were looking for the prophet like Moses who was promised in Deuteronomy 18:18–19. They would not likely realize that when John sent two of his disciples to ask Jesus, "Art thou he that should come or look we for another?"[7] it was unknown whether the Messiah and the "prophet like Moses" would be the same man. Without a foundation in Torah, many might not recognize that the Day of Pentecost[8] is the Feast of Weeks, *Shavuot*. *Shavuot* is found by counting seven Sabbaths from Firstfruit, beginning on the morning after the Sabbath immediately following Passover.[9] Seven weeks after the first day is the fiftieth day. *Pentekosta* in Greek means fiftieth. Later,[10] Paul is endeavoring to reach Jerusalem by "Pentecost," because *Shavuot* is a pilgrimage feast, where all adult male Israelites are required to present themselves before YHVH at the Temple.[11]

Jesus' Jewishness is the reason I use Hebraic forms of names in my brief. The Greek forms which may be more familiar to the reader carry a lot of Hellenized baggage. I also refer to early followers of Yeshua as "Nazarean," rather than "Nazarene," to distinguish

---

4. Keiser, *Pre-Christian*, 14.
5. Matt 9:19–22.
6. John 1:19–23.
7. Luke 7:19.
8. Acts 2:1.
9. Rabbinites count the day of Passover as the special sabbath and count from that holiday rather than from the first the weekly sabbath immediately following Passover Day. Saducees, many Messianics, and many Karaites observe Firstfruits on the Sunday after Passover. This method results in Shavuot always falling on Sunday; the rabbinic method allows Shavuot to fall on any day of the week.
10. Acts 20:16.
11. Deut 16:16.

The Nazareans

them from a modern denomination called the "Church of the Nazarene."

If we succeed in transporting ourselves in our imagination through time and space to late second Temple Judea, then what did the original movement look like? It was ethnically Jewish. They kept the Torah as Moses instructed, not according to the *takanot*[12] and *ma'asim*[13] of the Pharisees. They ate biblically kosher; they observed Sabbath and the Festivals of Yehovah. (Christmas and Easter would be foreign to them.) All that distinguished Nazarean Jews from the Jewish mainstream was the belief that Rabbi Yeshua bar Yosef is the Messiah.

As Jews, the Nazareans held fast to the absolute unity of their God, as stated in the *Shema*: "Hear, O Israel: The LORD our God *is* one LORD."[14] When a Scribe asked Yeshua which commandment was the greatest in the Law, the *Torah*, he answered:

> The first of all the commandments is, Hear, O Israel; The LORD our God is one LORD: And thou shalt love the LORD thy God with all thy heart, and with all thy soul, and with all thy mind, and with all thy strength: this is the first commandment. And the second is like, namely this, Thou shalt love thy neighbour as thyself. There is none other commandment greater than these.[15]

One means one. One does not mean three, or three-in-one. One means one. Many post-biblical Christians claim that one can mean a "compound unity," whatever that may mean. This is simply not correct translation. It is not exegesis, but eisegesis.

The early Nazareans were scrupulously Torah-observant.[16] Yeshua had taught:

> Think not that I am come to destroy the law, or the prophets: I am not come to destroy, but to fulfil. For

---

12. Lit. repair or correction of the Torah.
13. Rabbinic enactments, not found in the written Torah.
14. Deut 6:4.
15. Mark 12:29–31.
16. Priestley, *History*, 7.

verily I say unto you, Till heaven and earth pass, one jot or one tittle shall in no wise pass from the law, till all be fulfilled. Whosoever therefore shall break one of these least commandments, and shall teach men so, he shall be called the least in the kingdom of heaven: but whosoever shall do and teach them, the same shall be called great in the kingdom of heaven.[17]

Justo Gonzalez explains that the Nazareans "did not reject Judaism but were convinced that their faith was the fulfillment of the Messiah whom Jews over the ages had been anticipating. For this reason, Christians in Jerusalem continued to keep the Sabbath and attend worship at the Temple."[18]

Torah observant includes, among other things, eating biblically kosher, and keeping the feasts and Sabbath. Not a *yod* or a stroke will be deleted from Torah until all is fulfilled. Not until Messiah delivers the Kingdom to God the Father at the end of the Millennium[19] will "all" be fulfilled. Meanwhile, we have Torah for "instruction in right living."[20]

Remember Peter's vision. A Roman Centurion named Cornelius, a Gentile, had received a visit from an angel. The angel told him to send for Simon Peter, then staying in Joppa, to come and preach. He does so. Meanwhile,

> Peter went up upon the housetop to pray about the sixth hour:
> And he became very hungry, and would have eaten: but while they made ready, he fell into a trance,
> And saw heaven opened, and a certain vessel descending unto him, as it had been a great sheet knit at the four corners, and let down to the earth:
> Wherein were all manner of fourfooted beasts of the earth, and wild beasts, and creeping things, and fowls of the air.

17. Matt 5:17–19.
18. González, *Story*, 40.
19. 1 Cor 15:24.
20. 2 Tim 3:16.

The Nazareans

> And there came a voice to him, Rise, Peter; kill, and eat.
>
> But Peter said, Not so, Lord; for I have never eaten any thing that is common or unclean.
>
> And the voice *spake* unto him again the second time, What God hath cleansed, *that* call not thou common.
>
> This was done thrice: and the vessel was received up again into heaven.
>
> Now while Peter doubted in himself what this vision which he had seen should mean, behold, the men which were sent from Cornelius had made enquiry for Simon's house, and stood before the gate,[21]

Notice that Peter balks at the idea that he should eat unclean animals. He knows that Torah prohibits doing so. He did not believe that Torah had been abrogated. He continued to meditate on what the vision might mean.

He got his answer: "Of a truth I perceive that God is no respecter of persons: But in every nation he that feareth him, and worketh righteousness, is accepted with him."[22] It was not unclean animals that were declared clean, but Gentiles, people whom Judeans erroneously believed were inherently unclean.

Israelites are commanded to keep the Sabbath, "throughout their generations, *for* a perpetual covenant."[23] With terms like "perpetual," "forever," and "throughout their generations," we would not expect the commandment to expire. There is no language in this instruction to the effect of "but only until Messiah comes."

The biblical feasts are not "Jewish" holidays, they are Yehovah's feasts.[24] Those of the Nations who join themselves to the People of Israel are also invited. There is one Law for the homeborn and the stranger sojourning among the People.[25]

Nazarean Torah observance is different from Rabbinic observance. Yeshua had instructed his followers to "keep God's

21. Acts 10:9b–17.
22. Acts 10:34–35.
23. Ex 31:12–17.
24. Lev 23, Num 29:12, Deut 16, etc.
25. Exod 12:49.

commandments."²⁶ Keeping God's commandments demonstrates that we love God.²⁷ His commandments are not a burden,²⁸ but a delight.²⁹ We are warned to beware of "leaven of the Pharisees and Sadducees,"³⁰ which he defines as their doctrine. We are enjoined to "observe and do" what Moses commands, but not according to the *takanot*³¹ and *ma'asim*³² of the Pharisees.³³ Keeping God's commandments sometimes requires that we violate some human commandments.

---

26. Matt 19:17, John 14:15, 15:10.
27. 1 John 2:3, 3:22.
28. 1 John 5:3.
29. Ps 1:2, 40:8, 119:70, 77, 174, Rom 7:22.
30. Matt 16:11–12.
31. Lit. repair or correction of the Torah.
32. Rabbinic enactments, not found in the written Torah.
33. Matt 23:2.

Moses' Seat

MATTHEW REPORTS: "Then spake Jesus to the multitude, and to his disciples, Saying, The scribes and the Pharisees sit in Moses' seat: All therefore whatsoever they bid you observe, *that* observe and do; but do not ye after their works: for they say, and do not."[1] This appears to be an instruction to live by all the Pharisaical rules and regulations, contradicting Yeshua's practice of violating non-biblical rabbinic tradition. There is an error in transmission in this passage.

All the Greek texts of Matthew agree that Yeshua said ". . whatever *they* bid you observe . . . ." There is evidence that Matthew was originally written in Hebrew. In the Hebrew manuscripts, this passage has two variations. Some read "whatever *they* bid," and some read "whatever *he* bids." The difference in Hebrew between suffixes meaning "they" and "he" is one letter.[2] The reading " . . . whatever he (Moses) bids you observe . . . " avoids the contradiction which would result in rendering the verse " . . . whatever they [the Pharisees] bid you observe, but not according to [the Pharisees dogmas].

Rabbinic Judaism has piled rule upon rule, regulation upon regulation claiming that these rabbinic rulings were part of the "Oral Torah," derived from "Moses on Mount Sinai." The early Pharisees called their rules "the Tradition of the Elders." It was not

1. Matt 23:2.
2. ו *vav* for they; י *yod* for he. The two can easily be mistaken for each other.

the Pharisees who originally made the claim that these unwritten laws came down Mount Sinai with Moses, but the later Tannaim. It is common in Orthodox literature to find statements like, The Torah says X, but the Rabbis changed it to Y.[3] It is also common in Reform Jewish literature to find decisions to the effect that not only are the Rabbinic rules of *kashrut*, the dietary laws, not to be followed, but even the dietary instructions from Moses are superseded by modernity.[4]

We are not to follow extra-biblical regulations, "For they bind heavy burdens and grievous to be borne, and lay *them* on men's shoulders; but they *themselves* will not move them with one of their fingers."[5]

Pharisees, including "Pharisees which believed,"[6] accused Paul of abandoning Torah, because a) he followed the written Torah, but ceased following rabbinic ordinances, and b) people misunderstood his mission to the Gentiles.

Yeshua had said, "Don't think that I have come to destroy the Law."[7] and "Until heaven and earth pass away not the smallest letter nor the least stroke will be deleted from the Law,"[8] and "Whoever breaks the least commandment in the Law and teaches others to do the same will be called least in the Kingdom of God."[9] Inexplicably, from these and other sayings, most modern Christians conclude that the Law is abolished and that we should no longer keep any of the Commandments.

---

3. Schiffman, *Text*, 259.

4. From the Reform movement's Pittsburgh Platform of 1885: "We hold that all such Mosaic and Rabbinical laws as regulate diet, priestly purity, and dress originated in ages and under the influence of ideas altogether foreign to our present mental and spiritual state. They fail to impress the modern Jew with a spirit of priestly holiness; their observance in our days is apt rather to obstruct than to further modern spiritual elevation." My Jewish Learning, *Kashrut*.

5. Matt 23:4.
6. Acts 15:5.
7. Matt 5:17.
8. Matt 5:18.
9. Matt 5:19.

Moses' Seat

This is not how the early Nazarenes saw things. In Jerusalem, there were many thousands of Jews who believed, and were zealous for the Law.[10] Peter balked at the vision of four-footed animals, since he had never eaten anything unclean.[11] At James' suggestion, Paul underwent a Nazarite vow to prove that the reports of his abandoning Torah were false.[12] He may well have abandoned Pharisee *takanot* (Rabbinic rulings which purport to change the written Torah), but he never abandoned Torah.

Since heaven and earth have not passed away, we can conclude that the Creator's instructions in Torah have not passed away, either. When God, through Moses commanded, "Wherefore the children of Israel shall keep the sabbath, to observe the sabbath throughout their generations, *for* a perpetual covenant. It *is* a sign between me and the children of Israel for ever: for *in* six days the LORD made heaven and earth, and on the seventh day he rested, and was refreshed,"[13] Sabbath observance is required perpetually, not merely until Messiah comes. Passover is to be kept as an ordinance forever."[14] The feast of Unleavened Bread, *Chag ha-Matzot*, is commanded "by an ordinance forever."[15].

Antinomian Christians cite Colossians 2:14 to claim that Jesus "nailed the Law to his cross."

> Blotting out the handwriting of ordinances that was against us, which was contrary to us, and took it out of the way, nailing it to his cross;

"Ordinances" in the Greek is *dogma*, decrees. The Pharisees' "works" which we are to avoid in Matthew 23:2 above, is *ergon* in the Greek text and *takkanot* and *ma'asim* rendered "ordinances and deeds" in Howard's translation of Hebrew Matthew.[16] The

---

10. Acts 21:20.
11. Acts 10:14.
12. Acts 18:21–24.
13. Exod 31:16–17.
14. Exod 12:14.
15. Exod 12:17.
16. Howard, *Hebrew*, 112–13.

"handwriting of ordinances" is not God's instructions in Torah, but rules ordained by human religious leaders, handwriting of human hands. The Creator's instruction is not "against us," but for our good.[17]

"All scripture is given by inspiration of God, and is profitable for doctrine, for reproof, for correction, for instruction in righteousness:"[18] "All Scripture" includes, of course Torah. Since the New Testament was still being written when Paul wrote this part of the New Testament, Scripture can only mean *Tanakh*, the Hebrew Bible. Doctrine is right belief; reproof is for when we have erroneous beliefs; correction teaches us how to adjust our beliefs toward proper doctrine. Instruction in righteousness teaches us how to live correctly.

In Romans 11, Paul uses the analogy of a cultivated olive tree to represent the People of Israel. Some of the branches of this tree have broken off. There are certain sins in the Torah which result in the sinner being "cut off" from his people,[19] or to use Paul's analogy, pruned from the tree as deadwood. Gentiles who join themselves to Yehovah, keeping Sabbath and taking hold of the Covenant,[20] are grafted into the tree[21] and treated as though they were native born Israelites. There is to be one law for the stranger and the homeborn.[22] Those who join the "Commonwealth of Israel"[23] live by the same rules as everybody else. Thus, Paul advises us, "For whatsoever things were written aforetime were written for our learning, that we through patience and comfort of the scriptures might have hope."[24]

If Paul had taught that Torah was no longer in effect, then the Bereans who searched the *Tanakh* daily would have called him out

17. Deut 10:13.
18. 2 Tim 3:16.
19. Gen 17:14, Exod 12:15, 30:33, Lev 7:20, 7:27, etc.
20. Cf. Isaiah 56.
21. Rom 11:17–24.
22. Exod 12:49, Lev 24:22, Num 15:16, 29.
23. Cf. Eph 2:12.
24. Rom 15:4.

over proclaiming and end to those instructions which are forever. Some dispensationalists[25] claim that the present "Age of Grace" is entirely new, without precedent, that the entire dispensation is part of "the mystery which was kept secret since the world began."[26] If this were so, then the Bereans would have had nothing to search for in the Scriptures. There would be no mention of what would become Paul's teaching.[27]

As Paul tells us, "The Law is good, if a man use it lawfully."[28] Torah is not, and never has been a means of earning salvation. To try to perform enough *mitzvot*, commandments, to earn a place in the World to Come is an unlawful use of the Law, and only results in frustration. As Calvin said, "[T]he covenant, by which [the Jews] were united to the Lord, was founded, not on any merits of theirs, but on the mere mercy of God who called them."[29]

If God's people live according to His instruction, the *Goyim*, Gentiles, will be impressed and will want to get in on the benefits of a Torah-based lifestyle. Indeed, in late antiquity, the Greek and Roman gods were seen as capricious, arbitrary, self-serving, and generally unethical. By contrast, the God of Israel holds Himself to His covenants; He can be depended on. Sociologist Rodney Stark writes, "Judaism had long attracted 'fellow travelers,' who found much intellectual satisfaction in the moral teaching and monotheism of the Jews but would not take the final step of fulfilling the

---

25. "Dispensationalism" is the theory that God changes the rules from time to time. In the Garden of Eden, for example, there was only one rule: Do not eat the fruit of the Tree of Knowledge of Good and Evil. After the Flood, Noah and his descendants were given permission to eat animals, while taking care not to eat blood. For more information see Appendix 6.

26. Rom 16:25.

27. Many dispensationalists claim that the new covenant in this present "church" age is not with Israel, but with the "church," which is neither Jewish nor Gentile, but a new third classification. Jeremiah 31:31, (also quoted in Heb 8:8) proclaims Yehovah's promise that He will "make a new covenant with the House of Israel and with the House of Judah," not with a new entity.

28. 1 Tim 1:8.

29. Calvin, *Institutes*, 508.

Law."[30] In particular, the requirement of circumcision deterred many potential converts. "God-fearers," as these Gentile fellow travelers were called, were welcome in traditional synagogues, but only as associate members. The first generation of the Nazarean movement was still thoroughly Jewish, but received Gentile converts as full members, subject to minimal conditions.[31] They were expected to learn and adopt the practice of Torah gradually.[32] Unfortunately, the Greeks who were fascinated by this Hebrew, proto-Christianity were not as fascinated with the Scriptures.[33] This will have serious consequences later.

The Law teaches us what sin is.[34] Sin is the transgression of the Law.[35] The Law teaches us how to live a holy lifestyle,[36] [37] in response to our love for God,[38] since He loved us first.[39] Israel is called to be a light to the Nations;[40] those of the Nations who answer God's call are to be a light to the world. If we live in the same manner as the world, how will they see our light?

The believers in Colossae were told not to let anyone judge them in respect to food or holidays.[41] This is not because they had *quit* eating kosher and keeping Sabbath, but as converts from Greek polytheism, they had recently *begun* doing so, and their neighbors thought that they were crazy because of it. Also, the Pharisees, including the Pharisees who believed,[42] thought that these new Torah-observers were doing it wrong.

30. Stark, *Rise*, 58.
31. Acts 15:19–20.
32. Acts 15:21.
33. Hopkins, *Philosophy*, 75.
34. Rom 7:7.
35. 1 John 3:4.
36. Num 15:40.
37. My Jewish Learning, *Kashrut*.
38. 1 John 5:2–3.
39. 1 John 4:9.
40. Isa 42:6, 49:6, 51:4, 60:3.
41. Col 2:6.
42. Acts 15:5.

Moses' Seat

It was not for our benefit alone that God gave His people the Torah. It is His way of advertising.

> Behold, I [Moses] have taught you statutes and judgments, even as the LORD my God commanded me, that ye should do so in the land whither ye go to possess it.
>
> Keep therefore and do them; for this is your wisdom and your understanding in the sight of the nations, which shall hear all these statutes, and say, Surely this great nation is a wise and understanding people.
>
> For what nation is there so great, who hath God so nigh unto them, as the LORD our God is in all things that we call upon him for?
>
> And what nation is there so great, that hath statutes and judgments so righteous as all this law, which I set before you this day?
>
> Only take heed to thyself, and keep thy soul diligently, lest thou forget the things which thine eyes have seen, and lest they depart from thy heart all the days of thy life: but teach them thy sons, and thy sons' sons;[43]

If God's people live according to His instruction, the Gentiles will be impressed and will want to get in on the benefits of a Torah-based lifestyle. If the world sees God's people binding themselves with rules that God never commanded, who will want to join them?

The third of the Ten Commandments, "Thou shalt not take the name of the LORD thy God in vain; for the LORD will not hold him guiltless that taketh his name in vain,"[44] is not primarily about cussing. "Take" in Hebrew is *nasa*, bear or carry. We are not to bear the name of Yehovah in emptiness, vanity, falsehood. To bear the Name in vain includes claiming to be God's people, while not walking the talk, or inventing new rules which God never commanded and claiming that they are of divine origin. It also includes swearing falsely by God's Name, saying, "As the LORD liveth," as an oath and then not performing what was promised.

---

43. Deut 4:5–9.
44. Exod 20:7.

Our job is to advertise for the Kingdom by living the lifestyle of holiness as instructed in the Torah. We may not add to nor diminish from Yehovah's commands. This is how Yeshua walked; we are to follow his example.[45]

As we have said, living by Torah is not and never has been a means of earning salvation. Salvation is and has always been "by grace through faith."[46] Abraham, the "father of all who believe,"[47] "believed in the LORD." That is, he believed the words which Yehovah spoke to him and acted on those words. In Hebrew, the word translated "he believed" is *v'he'emin* from the root *aleph-mem-nun*, where we get the loan word Amen. We say Amen to a prayer or blessing, meaning that we agree that the words of the prayer or blessing are faithful. Maimonides' Thirteen Principles of Faith each begin with the phrase, "*Ani ma'amin b'emunah shlemah . . .* " "I believe with complete faith . . . " Abram's belief was not merely accepting the proposition that he would be the father of many nations and that his descendants would inherit the Promised Land. His belief led to faithful action, and Yehovah counted his faithfulness as righteousness.

Yeshua and his followers made a point violating man-made religious rules. The Pharisees, who held that the Oral Law rulings of Rabbinic Sages were equivalent in authority to the written Torah, naturally took offense.

---

45. 1 John 2:6.
46. Eph 2:8.
47. Rom 4:11.

Takanot Violated

Yeshua and his disciples went out of their way to violate Pharisee rules, while staying faithful to God's commandments delivered to the Israelites by Moses. Some of these are:

THRESHING

The Rabbis identify 39 species of *malakhah*, work which is prohibited on Sabbath. Threshing grain is one. The Rabbis consider rubbing grain with the hand to be threshing.[1] When Yeshua and his disciples picked grain in the field, they rubbed it with their hands to separate the grain from the stalk. It is lawful to pick grain on the Sabbath for immediate consumption. This is part of God's provision for the poor. The land belongs to the Creator, and He commands that the poor may eat from it as needed but may not take extra to save for later.[2]

While Yeshua's disciples were permitted by Torah to do as they did in this case, they transgressed the rabbinic "fence" around the Torah, which the Pharisees called lawbreaking.

---

1. Threshing is not limited to separating grain from chaff. Even wringing water out of your hair after showering is within the Rabbinic understanding of "threshing." My Jewish Learning, *Shower*.
2. Lev 19:10.

TAKE UP YOUR BED AND WALK

Jeremiah 17:19–22 prohibits carrying burdens into Jerusalem, on the Sabbath, presumably for purposes of commerce. Also forbidden is carrying a burden out of your houses on Shabbat. The Rabbis interpret this also to include carrying from outside to inside your home, crossing the boundary in either direction from public to private domain or private to public.

When Yeshua told the formerly paralyzed man to "take up your bed and walk," the man appeared to the Pharisees to be violating the rabbinic extension of the provision in Jeremiah. "The Jews therefore said unto him that was cured, It is the Sabbath day: it is not lawful for thee to carry thy bed."[3] He was not carrying his bed into the city, nor out of his house. He was taking it to his home. He was therefore not violating the instruction from Jeremiah, He was, however in violation of the Pharisees' enlargement of Jeremiah's prohibition.

WASH HANDS BEFORE EATING BREAD

Before eating bread, the tradition calls for a ritual handwashing accompanied by the blessing, "Blessed are You, YHVH our God, King of the universe, Who sanctified us by His commandments, and commanded us concerning washing of the hands."[4] There is no commandment in the written Torah about washing one's hands before eating bread. The traditional blessing before eating and the Grace after Meals[5] take one form before and after a meal which includes bread and a different form for a meal which does not include bread. These rituals are of strictly rabbinic origin; they are not in the written Torah.

The Pharisees challenged Yeshua asking, "Why do your disciples transgress the tradition of the elders by not washing their

---

3. John 5:10.

4. More literally, " . . . concerning lifting hands."

5. There is an example of Grace after Meals in Appendix 4, Shabbat Dinner.

Takanot Violated

hands when they eat bread?" He replied, "Why do you transgress the commandment of God by your traditions?"[6]

STONE JARS

In rabbinic literature, vessels made of stone are thought not to be susceptible to ritual contamination which would render them "unclean." Some materials, such as pottery, can retain the "taste" of what was stored in them. In that case, dishes used for meat would retain the taste of meat, and then could not be used for dairy. (The separation of meat and dairy is a rabbinic interpretation of the command not to "boil a kid [young goat] in its mother's milk.[7]) If a meat dish came in contact with dairy, or a dairy dish came in contact with meat, it would become unclean. While there are procedures for re-kashering some defiled vessels, a pottery dish must be broken and thrown out.

Stone vessels were thought to be incapable of becoming impure, therefore they were used to store water for purification rituals, such as handwashing before eating bread, or upon rising in the morning. Water for ritual purification must be "living," or moving water. Rain or a running stream is "moving" water and can be collected in stone cistern without losing its living character. This is a rabbinic, not Mosaic, rule.

Jesus' first miracle is told in John 2, the famous story of turning water into wine:

> And the third day there was a marriage in Cana of Galilee; and the mother of Jesus was there: And both Jesus was called, and his disciples, to the marriage. And when they wanted wine, the mother of Jesus saith unto him, They have no wine. Jesus saith unto her, Woman, what have I to do with thee? Mine hour is not yet come. His mother saith unto the servants, Whatsoever he saith unto you, do it. And there were set there six waterpots of stone, after the manner of the purifying of the Jews,

---

6. Matt 15:1–3.
7. Exod 12:19, 34:26, Deut 14:21.

containing two or three firkins apiece. Jesus saith unto them, Fill the waterpots with water. And they filled them up to the brim. And he saith unto them, Draw out now, and bear unto the governor of the feast. And they bare it. When the ruler of the feast had tasted the water that was made wine, and knew not whence it was: (but the servants which drew the water knew;) the governor of the feast called the bridegroom, And saith unto him, Every man at the beginning doth set forth good wine; and when men have well drunk, then that which is worse: but thou hast kept the good wine until now.[8]

This short narrative is jam-packed with significant information. Yeshua and his disciples attend a wedding in Cana, which is close to his hometown of Nazareth. His mother reports that they had run out of wine. His response in the original is much more respectful than it looks in the King James Version, "Ma'am, why are you telling me? It's not my turn."

A wedding feast could last ten days.[9] This would require a great deal of wine. Male guests would contribute wine to the party in descending order of seniority. Since Jesus was relatively young, "about thirty,"[10] it was not yet his turn to supply the wine.[11] Mary ignores his objection and tells the wait staff to "Do whatever he says."

Jesus tells the servants to top-off the jars. Since the ritually pure water was already in the jars, they would have had to top them off with "ordinary" water. This may or may not have caused the ritual defilement of the pure water; there is a rabbinic rule which allows a *de minimus* contamination in most matters.

Once the pure water had been turned into wine, the host's household no longer had ritually pure water for ablutions.

---

8. John 2:1–10.
9. Pillai, *Light*, 16.
10. Luke 3:23.
11. Pillai, *Light*, 13.

Takanot Violated

By putting wine into the stone water jars, Yeshua violated rabbinic *halachah*, but transgressed no actual law whatsoever in the written Torah.

THREE VERSES

There is a Rabbinic rule that when the Scriptures are read publicly, the reader should read at least three verses. This is to keep what is read in context. This rule, I think, is good advice. As we have said, "when you take the text out of the context, all you have left is the 'con.'"

As good as this advice may be, it is not a Torah rule. Yeshua specifically violated it in the one time it is recorded that he read Scripture in the synagogue:

> And he came to Nazareth, where he had been brought up: and, as his custom was, he went into the synagogue on the sabbath day, and stood up for to read. And there was delivered unto him the book of the prophet Esaias. And when he had opened the book, he found the place where it was written,
>
> The Spirit of the Lord *is* upon me, because he hath anointed me to preach the gospel to the poor; he hath sent me to heal the brokenhearted, to preach deliverance to the captives, and recovering of sight to the blind, to set at liberty them that are bruised,
>
> To preach the acceptable year of the Lord.
>
> And he closed the book, and he gave *it* again to the minister, and sat down. And the eyes of all them that were in the synagogue were fastened on him. And he began to say unto them, This day is this scripture fulfilled in your ears.[12]

All eyes were on him, as Luke tells us, in part because he had just violated the three-verse rule by stopping in the middle of the second verse. Isaiah goes on to say " . . . and the day of vengeance of our God." But Yeshua stopped when he did because he was

---

12. Luke 4:16–21.

proclaiming the "acceptable year," and not the Day of Vengeance, which is still future.

EATING WITH SINNERS

Yeshua famously ate with publicans and sinners. A publican was a tax collector. He would typically be a local who collaborated with the occupying Roman government. He would buy his position from the authorities and squeeze as much money out of the people as he could, expecting to make a tidy profit. Essentially, he had a license to rob.

Sinners, to the *Parushim*, Pharisees, were fellow Jews who were not sufficiently observant. They didn't keep kosher *enough*; they didn't keep the Sabbath strictly *enough*. The Pharisee party were *parush*, separate. They kept themselves from those whose sense of purity did not come up to their standards. Keep in mind that this is not all bad. Paul recommends that we "have no fellowship with the unfruitful works of darkness, but rather reprove them."[13] The Pharisees had gotten their purity out of balance. It is not a sin to be ritually impure.[14] One must become pure before entering the Temple, however. The Pharisees tried to maintain their state of purity uninterrupted.

Remember that when Peter went as instructed to the house of Cornelius, he says, that, "Ye know how that it is an unlawful thing for a man that is a Jew to keep company, or come unto one of another nation . . . "[15] This is not written in the Torah but was part of the tradition of the elders. He goes on to say, " . . . but God hath shewed me that I should not call any man common or unclean." In this he followed the example of his master by violating tradition to do what he was actually commanded.

---

13. Eph 5:11.

14. Remember that a woman in menses is ritually impure and forbidden to her husband until her purity is regained. Still, menstruation is not "sin," it is the natural process of the Creator's design.

15. Acts 10:28.

Nazarean Lifestyle

THE MIRACULOUS HEALINGS as reported in the Book of Acts were not specific to the Nazarean movement. In Rabbinic literature, Choni the Circle Drawer was probably the best-known miracle worker of the first century BCE. When the land was in need of rain, according to legend, the leaders of the people would come to Choni to pray for rain. In perhaps the most famous incident, the one that gave him his nickname, he drew a circle on the ground and prayed for rain, vowing not to leave the circle until a gentle, soaking rain came.[1] The rains came as he had prayed.

The Hebrew culture of the day thought of miracles as the natural order of how God created the universe. Mark reports that the Lord confirmed the Apostles teaching with signs.[2] Miraculous expectation was so high that people received healing even if nothing more than Simon Peter's shadow fell on them.[3] Also in Acts, people were held in thrall by non-believing wonder workers; Simon the Sorcerer[4] and the seven sons of Sciva[5] are mentioned by name.

They gathered daily. They ate their meals together. There were no social distinctions among them, at least ideally. Supervisors/pastors/elders led by example; they did not rule by decree. They

1. Chabad, *Choni*.
2. Mark 16:20.
3. Acts 5:15.
4. Acts 8:9–11.
5. Acts 19:13.

took care of each other, each recognizing that their assets were God's property to be used for His Kingdom; the legal owners were merely stewards, trustees.[6]

When disciples met, Dunn tells us:

> It is important to recognize how distinctive the practice of earliest Christian worship was. Prayers were said and hymns sung; to that extent earliest Christian gatherings conformed to the regular practice of worship in other cults. Nevertheless, their gatherings for worship and for shared meals were unique. Unlike any other cult or club, there was no sacred space in which they met, no far-off Temple towards which they directed their worship. Their sacred time was different and distinct, their sacred meal allowed no comparison or competitor. There were no priests present to officiate and to render their meals acceptable or their worship possible. No sacrifices were offered; there were no libations to any god. Onlookers might well wonder whether this *was* a cult, whether their gatherings were religious, as the practice of religion was generally understood.[7]

Their common meals would have looked more like a potluck, than a "service," more like Sunday Dinner than a Eucharist, more like a Friday evening Shabbat table than a Mass.[8]

They had neither dedicated sacred space nor a clergy class. There were elders, to be sure, but they were not an elite. Ministries of apostles, prophets, evangelists, pastors and teachers were present,[9] but again, these were not a priestly class. They were simply fellow disciples who served in their respective callings.

Each assembly was autonomous but associated with other like gatherings. A member's living room was the practical limit to the size of a local group. They all participated, as the spirit directed, there were no rows of pews filled with spectators watching

---

6. Jacomb-Hood, *Rediscovering*, Chapter 7.

7. Dunn, *Worship*, 57, emphasis in the original.

8. For a simplified description of a typical Shabbat dinner in a Jewish home, see Appendix 4: Shabbat Dinner.

9. Eph 4:11.

the trained professionals perform. The manifestation of the spirit was in evidence. The gift ministries operated to edify and helped maintain unity.

Christian Drift

As we have noted, the original Jesus Movement was entirely Jewish, with a Hebraic mind set, a Hebrew manner of thinking and speaking, and came from a culture steeped in the Hebrew Scriptures, the *Tanakh*, which Christians call the "Old" Testament.

Beginning with the incident at the home of Cornelius the centurion,[1] Gentiles began joining the movement, as Gentile believers, without converting to Judaism. These early Gentile converts were "God-fearers," a name given to non-Jews who were part of the Jewish community. They were part of synagogue life. They had been drawn to Judaism from the polytheism of their Greek culture by its ethos and intellectual rigor.

The local synagogue was more a community center and municipal building than a specifically religious center. It was at the hub of village activity. Like the New England colonial meeting house, it was used for all kinds of gatherings: courts, weddings, communal meals. As municipal centers, synagogues were not affiliated with any particular sect. Like the parish church in Catholic Europe before the Reformation, it was the center of the life of the community. Most Catholics are simply Catholic and not affiliated with the Dominicans, the Franciscans, or the Benedictines. In the late second temple era, most Jews were simply Jews, and not affiliated with the Pharisees, the Sadducees, or the Essenes.

As a result of Gentiles joining the movement, the leadership in Jerusalem met to consider what conditions of membership to

1. Acts 10:1–11:18.

Christian Drift

require of them. After much deliberation, the decision was made that Gentile disciples need to "abstain from pollutions of idols, and *from* fornication, and *from* things strangled, and *from* blood."[2] These four things were not the sum total of everything a Gentile believer needed to do; this was the minimum requirement for admission. It was expected that they would learn Torah gradually as they continued to hear the weekly readings in the synagogue. As James continued, "For Moses of old time hath in every city them that preach him, being read in the synagogues every sabbath day."

Hearing Torah read weekly is also a minimum. Remember that Luke praised the believers in Berea for searching the Scriptures daily.[3] Due to his background, many say that Paul had the entire *Tanakh* memorized.[4] Some say only that he had the Torah memorized.[5] At the very least, he was extremely well versed in the Scriptures. References to the Hebrew Bible are scattered liberally throughout his New Testament writings.

Paul also encouraged his students to imitate him the way he imitated Messiah.[6] Rabbinic tradition also holds that each person has an obligation to "attend the House of Study daily."[7] House of Study, *Beit Midrash*, is a synonym for synagogue.

In modern missiological terms, the process of evangelizing and discipling is called "indignation" and "pilgrimization." The

---

2. Acts 15:6–20.

3. Acts 17:11.

4. DeWeese, *Exegesis*.

5. In some synagogues in the present day, there is a paid professional Torah reader. The text is divided into 55 weekly portions. The Torah is read from a hand-written scroll. There are no vowels, punctuation marks or musical notations in a kosher scroll. To prepare, a reader memorizes the week's text out of a *Tikkun*, a book where the text as it appears in a Torah scroll will be on one side of the page, and the "vocalized" text is on the other with vowel points and cantillation marks. In this way, one who is expert in this skill, and who delivers the public readings frequently, will soon memorize large chunks of Torah. After some years, he may have the entire Torah memorized. In other congregations, volunteer readers may read excerpts. These readers are less likely to have memorized the whole Torah.

6. 1 Cor 11:1.

7. Scherman, *Siddur*, 19.

Apostles first made the Message accessible to the indigenous Gentile population, by explaining it in terms they could understand. Then, they led the new converts to learn to conform to God's requirements, making pilgrims of them.

The charge levelled at "seeker friendly" churches is that they leave people perpetually in the "pew-warmer" stage and never teach them the Walk, never say anything to make anyone uncomfortable. It is said that they indigenize, but never pilgrimize.

There were no specifically Nazarean synagogues "from old time." Nazarean Jews and God-fearers would be part of a local synagogue community, along with all other Jews, while the Movement was still a welcome part of the Israelite people. There would be regular gatherings for prayer and study in those days as is the case today.

Nazareans and Pharisees (and others) mingled in the same congregations, at least for a while. It is commonly thought that this fact is supported by the existence of the *Birkat ha-Minim*. This "blessing," which is not in fact a blessing, but a curse against heretics, was added to the *Shmoneh-esrei*, the "Eighteen Benedictions" of the Weekday *Amidah*, or "Standing Prayer," the central part of the daily liturgy. Also referred to as *ha-Tefilah*, "*The* Prayer," the *Shmoneh-esrei* was developed after the destruction of the Temple, and possibly by Rabban Gamliel at Yavne.

It is commonly thought that the *Birkat ha-Minim* was composed to weed out Nazareans and other heretics. It is assumed that a member of a *minyan*, a gathering of at least ten Jewish men for prayer, who is invited to lead the service on any given day would not want to pronounce a curse on himself and would be exposed if he balked at reciting that *bracha* (blessing). The text of the Blessing is:

> May no hope be left to the slanderers; but may wickedness perish as in a moment; may all Thine enemies be soon cut off, and do Thou speedily uproot the haughty and shatter and humble them speedily in our days.

Christian Drift

Blessed be Thou, O LORD, who strikest down enemies and humblest the haughty.[8]

Perceiving a need and composing a prayer to be added to a fixed ritual takes time. It was not in place on the Sabbath immediately following Pentecost. Also, a Nazarean would not think himself to be a heretic or "wanton sinner."

Daniel Boyerin casts doubt on this theory of the origin of the *Birkat ha-Minim*.[9] He writes that the earliest mention of the "blessing" is in the Tosefta, mid third century. There is a suggestion that it was directed, not so much at the Nazareans, but at the Pharisees. "Pharisee" comes from *parush*, separate. The Pharisees separated themselves from the public mainstream as an attempt to maintain a state of ritual purity continuously. This separation was seen as endangering the unity of the Jewish People.

The final split between the Nazareans and the Rabbinites may have come when Rabbi Akiva declared Shimon bar Kosiba to be the Messiah *circa* 135CE, renaming him Bar Kochba, "Son of a Star." According to legend, Nazareans left the rebel army in droves, rather than to fight under a banner of any messiah other than Yeshua. Though, as mentioned above in the Introduction, Epiphanius mentions "Nasaraeans" (*sic*) as a sect of Judaism as late as the fourth century.[10] There was no sudden, universal break. There was no individual nor committee in either movement with the authority to decree such a break.

Gentile converts to the Nazarean Movement were grafted into the olive tree which represents Israel;[11] they did not replace Israel. They undertook to live by the Law, as there is to be only one law for the stranger and native born alike.[12] Gentiles being "grafted in" to the People of Israel is identical to the "mixed multitude" of

---

8. Adler and Hirsch, *Shemoneh*. See also Scherman, *Siddur*, 113.
9. Boyerin, *Justin*, 427–61.
10. Carlson, *Development*, 5.
11. Rom 11:17–21.
12. Exod 12:49, Num 15:16, 29.

Gentiles who joined the Hebrews in the Exodus,[13] and became part of Israel. They continued in the Apostles doctrine, built on the foundation of the Law and Prophets. They did not lift the Gospel of John or the Letter to the Ephesians out of their contexts (neither of which had yet been written) and hang their dogmas from them.

Christian antinomians claim that the four rules propounded by the council of elders in Jerusalem are the only rules incumbent on Gentile Christians. Do they suggest that stealing and perjury and dishonoring one's parents are now acceptable? They do claim that Sabbath breaking is now not only permitted, but is virtually mandatory, since the Church moved its weekly observance from the seventh day of the week to the first.

Some years later, a great influx of Gentiles began as a result of the ministry of Paul. It was in Antioch, Syria that the disciples were first called Christians.[14] They were not Nazarean Jews, because they were not Jewish. These Greek disciples were accepted as full members in this Jewish Nazarean sect without having to undergo circumcision, as they would have been required to do to become full members of the larger Jewish mainstream. The great numbers of Greek-speaking Gentiles tipped the balance in the movement away from a Hebrew culture to a Hellenized one. These converts were not as familiar with the Hebrew Scriptures as their predecessors among the God-fearers brought into the faith under the ministry of Simon Peter, some years before.[15]

A Hebrew mind set is indispensable to an understanding of the Bible. As John Dillenberger wrote, "[T]o ignore Hebraic ways of thinking is to subvert Christian understanding."[16] Yet from the second century on, the Hellenized church not only ignored Hebraic thought, but actively sought to purge the Church of all things even remotely Jewish.

Before the New Testament writings were even written, however, never mind canonized, nearly everyone forsook the teaching

13. Exod 12:38.
14. Acts 11:26.
15. Acts 10.
16. Dillenberger, *Revelational*, 159–75.

Christian Drift

and went after "some other Jesus,"[17] once again leaving only a remnant. While Paul, the Apostle to the Gentiles[18] was still writing, he warned Gentile converts, "Beware lest any man spoil you through philosophy and vain deceit, after the tradition of men, after the rudiments of the world, and not after Christ."[19] Greek culture was as steeped in Plato as Jewish culture was steeped in Moses.

As we have seen, educated Greek converts ignored Paul's warning and brought Greek philosophy with them as they joined the Nazarean Movement.

Alister McGrath, in his *Historical Theology*, writes:

> The study of the history of theology suggests that Christianity can sometimes unconsciously absorb ideas and values from its cultural backdrop. Certain ideas which have often been regarded as distinctively Christian sometimes turn out to be borrowed from a secular context. The idea that God cannot suffer was well established in Greek philosophical circles. Early Christian theologians, *anxious to gain respect and credibility* in such circles, did not challenge this idea. As a result, it became deeply embedded in the Christian theological tradition.[20]

It was this "other Jesus" that eventually became mainstream. Within 300 years, this "other Jesus" was the center of the official universal religion of the Roman Empire. Bishops were lords over God's people. Greek philosophy replaced the Hebrew Torah. Eating pork was mandatory. Sabbath was moved from the seventh day of the week, Saturday, to the first, Sunday.

For seventeen centuries, Nicene Christianity and Rabbinic Judaism have been repelling each other, like galaxies accelerating away from each other under the influence of "dark energy," in an ever-growing rift, competing for acceptance as the true heirs of the

---

17. Cf. 2 Cor 11:4.
18. Rom 11:13, 1 Tim 2:7, 2 Tim 1:11.
19. Col 2:8 "Spoil" is *sulagogon*, meaning to carry away as a captive or as booty. "To the victor go the spoils." This is not an unruly child, a "spoiled brat," or food gone bad, as spoiled milk.
20. McGrath, *Historical*, 12, emphasis added.

faith of Abraham. Since the fourth century CE, the two movements have each been defining themselves, *inter alia*, as not the other. But if we draw a straight line through time from Abraham, through Moses and the prophets, past King David to Jesus of Nazareth, we arrive at neither Rabbinic Judaism nor Nicene Christianity, but at the "Sect of the Nazarenes."[21] They were Torah-observant, but not in the *halachah* of the Pharisees. They developed their own style of *kashrut* (dietary regulations) and *shechitah* (proper slaughter of edible animals),[22] independent of the Rabbis. They followed Yeshua, but not in the manner of the later Greek speculation of church councils.

Wolfram Kinzig tells us, "Apart from the relatively scarce remarks preserved by Epiphanius and Jerome, the Nazoraeans (*sic*) are rarely mentioned and cannot, therefore, have had a strong influence on the mainstream church."[23] This is not, I suggest, because the Nazareans were an obscure heretical sect, but because they continued in the teachings of Yeshua and his apostles, while the mainstream church severed itself from its roots. By the time of Constantine, the Empire did not "convert to Christianity." Rather, it re-branded Roman State Religion *as* "Christianity."

When Rome destroyed Jerusalem, the Nazareans escaped to Pella, Rabbi Yochanan ben Zakkai founded the Rabbinic Academy at Yavne to preserve Jewish learning, and Antioch became the unofficial headquarters of the Greek-speaking Gentile church. The Nazareans were persecuted by both the Bishops and the Rabbis. They inhabited a no-man's-land between them. Frequently, they had to go underground. But they never went extinct. For example, Ray Pritz[24] says that Nazarean Judaism disappeared in the fourth

---

21. Cf. Acts 24:5.

22. For example, Orthodox Jewish dietary rules presume that all meat has been sacrificed to idols and is therefore not kosher, unless it was processed from slaughter to retail sale under rabbinic supervision. When these rules were formulated, that was a reasonable presumption. In contrast, in 1 Cor 8, Paul takes a "don't ask, don't tell" attitude about provenance of meat which may or may not have been a sacrifice.

23. Kinzig, *Nazoraeans*, 463–87.

24. Pritz, *Nazarene*, 1.

century CE, but David Rudolph says, "The Second Council of Nicaea in 787 was the first ecumenical council to ban Messianic Jews from the church."[25] Clearly, some form of Jewish practice within Christianity still existed at least that late. Indeed, "Crypto-Jews" pop up from time to time throughout church history.[26] Descendants of Iberian Crypto-Jews who fled to the New World from the Inquisition still maintain customs of Jewish origin to this day, sometimes unwittingly.[27]

Emmanuel Tremellius was an Italian Jew who converted to Christianity about 1540, migrated to the Reformed Church and became known as one of the earliest Protestant Hebraists. He never gave up his Jewish identity, calling himself both a Christian and a Jew.[28] The Moravian Brethren tried to revive Nazarean Judaism with the *Judenkehille*, "Jewish community," in the 18th Century. The Nazarean movement, under various names, resurfaces from time to time, and though it may be sometimes hard to find, continues to this day.

Biblical accuracy will rarely, if ever, be mainstream. But the Creator will always have a remnant preserved to carry on the mission of bringing light to the world. When Elijah thought he was the last faithful one left, Yehovah tells him that there were 7,000 who had not knelt to Baal.[29] The true path is narrow, and few will find it,[30] but there will always be some who do.

As the Movement lost its Hebrew character, Greek philosophical ideas gained preeminence. The reader will remember that when Paul was summoned before the Sanhedrin, he used the rift between the Pharisees and Sadducees to his advantage. The Pharisees believed in a general resurrection and judgment at the end of

---

25. Rudolph, *Messianic*, 25.

26. While Crypto-Jews were not intentionally keeping the ancient Nazarean movement alive, they were a Jewish influence in the church, even when it was life threatening to be such.

27. Lipsitt, *Secret*.

28. Johnson, *Brethren*, iv.

29. 1 Kgs 19:18.

30. Matt 7:14.

days, while the Sadducees believed that there was no resurrection, but that the dead were dead forever. Rabbinic Judaism inherited the belief in resurrection, which was normative until modern times. The *Gevurot* section of the *Amidah*, the central prayer of Jewish liturgy still praises God "Who revives the dead [in the resurrection at the last day]."[31] Remember that Lazarus' sister Martha knew that her brother would "rise again in the resurrection at the last day."[32]

The Greek idea of an immortal soul was imported with the influx of Gentile converts. It had been unknown in Judaism, except for some peripheral syncretism in the diaspora. It was Plato, circa 350 BCE, who popularized the idea of an immortal soul.

Until the Hellenistic era, Hebrew thought held that the cure for death is resurrection, not immediate afterlife. Death is analogized as sleep.

- Daniel 12:2; "And many of them that sleep in the dust of the earth shall awake, some to everlasting life, and some to shame and everlasting contempt."
- Deuteronomy 31:16 God told Moses, "Thou shalt sleep with thy fathers."
- II Samuel 7:12 God tells David, "And when thy days be fulfilled, and thou shalt sleep with thy fathers . . . ."
- I Kings 2:10 says, "so David slept with his fathers, and was buried in the city of David."
- Job 7:21, Job says, " . . . for now shall I sleep in the dust . . . ."
- Psalm 13:3, Consider and hear me, O LORD my God: lighten mine eyes, lest I sleep the sleep of death.
- John 11:11–14 These things said he: and after that he saith unto them, Our friend Lazarus sleepeth; but I go, that I may awake him out of sleep. Then said his disciples, Lord, if he sleep, he shall do well. Howbeit Jesus spake of his death: but

---

31. Scherman, *Siddur*, 5.
32. John 11:24.

they thought that he had spoken of taking of rest in sleep. Then said Jesus unto them plainly, Lazarus is dead.

Job also tells us that resurrection is at the end of days:

> But man dieth, and wasteth away: yea, man giveth up the ghost, and where is he? As the waters fail from the sea, and the flood decayeth and drieth up: So man lieth down, and riseth not: till the heavens be no more, they shall not awake, nor be raised out of their sleep.[33]

Of course, sleep also means sleep.

When we fall asleep at night, we are not conscious of the passage of time. Unless sleep is interrupted, once asleep, the next conscious thought is waking in the morning. So it is with death and resurrection. When we fall asleep in death, the next conscious thought will be whatever resurrection we may be a part of, at which point we will stand before whichever judgment our resurrection precedes.

Yeshua told his disciples:

> Marvel not at this: for the hour is coming, in the which all that are in the graves shall hear his voice, And shall come forth; they that have done good, unto the resurrection of life; and they that have done evil, unto the resurrection of damnation. I can of mine own self do nothing: as I hear, I judge: and my judgment is just; because I seek not mine own will, but the will of the Father which hath sent me.[34]

Notice two resurrections in that teaching, a resurrection of life and a resurrection of damnation.[35] John tells us that these two resurrections are a thousand years apart.

> And I saw thrones, and they sat upon them, and judgment was given unto them: and I saw the souls of them that were beheaded for the witness of Jesus, and for the word of God, and which had not worshipped the beast, neither his image, neither had received his mark upon

---

33. Job 14:12.
34. John 5:28–30.
35. "Damnation" is *krisis* in Greek, usually translated "judgment."

their foreheads, or in their hands; and they lived and reigned with Christ a thousand years.

But the rest of the dead lived not again until the thousand years were finished. This is the first resurrection.

Blessed and holy is *he that hath part in the first resurrection: on such the second death hath no power*, but they shall be priests of God and of Christ, and shall reign with him a thousand years. And when the thousand years are expired, Satan shall be loosed out of his prison, And shall go out to deceive the nations which are in the four quarters of the earth, Gog and Magog, to gather them together to battle: the number of whom is as the sand of the sea.

And they went up on the breadth of the earth, and compassed the camp of the saints about, and the beloved city: and fire came down from God out of heaven, and devoured them.

And the devil that deceived them was cast into the lake of fire and brimstone, where the beast and the false prophet are, and shall be tormented day and night for ever and ever.

And I saw a great white throne, and him that sat on it, from whose face the earth and the heaven fled away; and there was found no place for them.

And I saw the dead, small and great, stand before God; and the books were opened: and another book was opened, which is the book of life: and the dead were judged out of those things which were written in the books, according to their works.

And the sea gave up the dead which were in it; and death and hell delivered up the dead which were in them: and they were judged every man according to their works.

And death and hell were cast into the lake of fire. This is the second death. And whosoever was not found written in the book of life was cast into the lake of fire.[36]

Some will quote the verse, "It is appointed to man once to die, and after this the judgment.[37]" They infer that the judgment

---

36. Rev 20:4–15, emphasis added.
37. Heb 9:27.

Christian Drift

comes *immediately* after death. "After" could be immediately after, or it could be some unspecified time after. "Immediately" is not in the text. Judgment, as we see, comes after the resurrection. No one goes directly from his deathbed to judgment. This is no proof text for an immediate afterlife nor for an "immortal soul."

Yeshua promises the penitent man on the next cross over, "Verily I say unto thee, To day shalt thou be with me in paradise."[38] This verse is mispunctuated. In the oldest manuscripts, there were no punctuation marks. Commas and periods reflect the opinion of the translators. Depending on the translator's belief about afterlife or resurrection it can be rendered "Verily I say to you today, 'You will be with me in Paradise,'" or "Verily I say to you, 'Today you will be with me in Paradise.'" The principle of non-contradiction suggests, "I say today, you will [in the future at the resurrection] be with me."

The usual use of "today" for emphasis also suggests the "I say today" rendering. Abraham's servant, on his quest to find Isaac a wife prayed, "Send me good speed this day . . . "[39] When Esau was hungry, Jacob said, "Sell me this day thy birthright;"[40] "And Laban said, This heap is a witness between me and thee this day. Therefore was the name of it called Galeed."[41] When Pharaoh could not remember and understand his dream, "Then spake the chief butler unto Pharaoh, saying, I do remember my faults this day."[42] We are instructed to "Know therefore this day, and consider it in thine heart, that the LORD he is God in heaven above, and upon the earth beneath: there is none else."[43]

The term "immortal soul" appears nowhere in the scripture, neither the *Tanakh* nor the New Testament. On the contrary, "the soul that sins, it will die."[44]

38. Luke 23:43.
39. Gen 24:12.
40. Gen 25:53.
41. Gen 31:48.
42. Gen 41:9.
43. Deut 4:39.
44. Ezek 18:4.

Neither Yavne nor Antioch

Many Evangelicals will recite, as though it were Scripture, "You are a spirit, you have a soul, and you live in a body." This statement also appears nowhere in the Bible, and is supported only by tradition, not text.

In Genesis, Elohim forms the man, the *adam*, the human, from the dust of the ground. Breathes into his nostrils the *neshama*, breath, of life, and the *adam* became a living soul, a living *nephesh*.[45] The *adam*, the human, *is* a *nephesh*, a soul. The human *is* also a physical body, made of dust.

Leviticus 17:11 tells us "The life of the flesh is in the blood." If enough blood is drained from the body, both the body and the life in the blood will die.

Yeshua's early disciples also looked forward to resurrection, and not immediate afterlife. When Yeshua went to raise Lazarus,

> Then said Martha unto Jesus, Lord, if thou hadst been here, my brother had not died. But I know, that even now, whatsoever thou wilt ask of God, God will give it thee.
> Jesus saith unto her, Thy brother shall rise again.
> Martha saith unto him, I know that he shall rise again in the resurrection at the last day.[46]

As late as the Council of Constantinople in 381CE, where the Nicene Creed was amended, resurrection of the dead was still an orthodox doctrine. "I believe in one God . . . And I look for the Resurrection of the dead: And the Life of the world to come."[47]

Bullinger puts the difference between truth and tradition in a nutshell:

> There is no article of the Christian Faith that has been more affected and injured by tradition than the hope of Resurrection. Notwithstanding the fact that there is no truth more important or more fundamental to the Gospel, there is none more neglected. It is difficult to find a

---

45. Gen 2:7.

46. John 11:21–24. Notice that Martha does not call him God, but expresses confidence that whatever Yeshua asks God for, God will give him.

47. Suter, *Common*, 71.

Christian Drift

hymn in any book which we can sing concerning this blessed hope. We can find hymns about Christ's resurrection, plenty about "Easter," but how few concerning the blessed fact that His people, who died with Him, have risen also in Him: how few about "the resurrection of the body," in which all profess to believe![48]

Justin Martyr, writing in the middle of the second century, affirms resurrection of the dead as a salvation issue:

> For I made it clear to you that those who are Christians in name, but in reality are godless and impious heretics, teach in all respects what is blasphemous and godless and foolish . . . . For even if you yourselves have ever met with some so-called Christians, who yet do not acknowledge this, but even dare to blaspheme the God of Abraham, and the God of Isaac, and the God of Jacob, who say too that there is no resurrection of the dead, but that their souls ascend to heaven at the very moment of their death-do not suppose that they are Christians, any more than if one examined the matter rightly he would acknowledge as Jews those who are Sadducees, or similar sects of Genistae, and Meristae, and Galileans, and Hellelians, and Pharisees and Baptists (pray, do not be vexed with me as I say all I think), but (would say) that though called Jews and children of Abraham, and acknowledging God with their lips, as God Himself has cried aloud, yet their heart is far from Him (Dialogue 80.3-4).[49]

For Justin, those "who say too that there is no resurrection of the dead, but that their souls ascend to heaven at the very moment of their death," are not Christians at all. Yet, to many Christians today, immediate afterlife is a fundamental doctrine.

Paul emphatically describes the necessity of resurrection:

> Now if Christ be preached that he rose from the dead, how say some among you that there is no resurrection of the dead? But if there be no resurrection of the dead, then is Christ not risen: And if Christ be not risen, then

---

48. Bullinger, *Hope*.
49. Justin, *Dialogue*, 453.

is our preaching vain, and your faith is also vain. Yea, and we are found false witnesses of God; because we have testified of God that he raised up Christ: whom he raised not up, if so be that the dead rise not. For if the dead rise not, then is not Christ raised: And if Christ be not raised, your faith is vain; ye are yet in your sins. Then they also which are fallen asleep in Christ are perished. If in this life only we have hope in Christ, we are of all men most miserable. But now is Christ risen from the dead, and become the firstfruits of them that slept. For since by man came death, by man came also the resurrection of the dead. For as in Adam all die, even so in Christ shall all be made alive.[50]

The fact that Messiah died also proves that he cannot be God. God is immortal; He cannot die. Trinitarians allege that Messiah must be "God incarnate" to qualify to be Messiah. This is an inference drawn by human committees. Yet again, this notion appears nowhere in Scripture. This passage clearly calls Messiah a man. Whatever his other qualifications may be, it is necessary that he be a human, "the Last Adam."[51] If he were God, then he did not die. If he did not die, he was not raised from the dead. If he was not raised from the dead, then the conditions for salvation in Romans[52] are false.

Since Koine Greek does not use an indefinite article, we could supply it and render verse 21 " . . . by *a* man came death, by *a* man came also the resurrection . . . " The man by whom resurrection came was, of course, empowered to do so as the Creator's *shaliach*, His agent.

The damage done by the importation of Platonic thought cannot be overstated. Greek philosophy's influence on developing Christianity is well known in academia but is little known

---

50. 1 Cor 15:12–22.

51. 1 Cor 15:45.

52. Rom 10:9 That if thou shalt confess with thy mouth the Lord Jesus, and shalt believe in thine heart that God hath raised him from the dead, thou shalt be saved.

Christian Drift

in the pews.[53] James Strong writes, "Towards the end of the 1st century, and during the 2nd, many learned men came over both from Judaism and paganism to Christianity. These brought with them into the Christian schools of theology their Platonic ideas and phraseology."[54]

Gibbon, in his *History of Christianity* exposes the Greek influence on the evolution of the Trinity, for example, saying "If Paganism was conquered by Christianity, it is equally true that Christianity was corrupted by Paganism. The pure Deism [basic religion, in this context] of the first Christians . . . was changed, by the Church of Rome, into the incomprehensible dogma of the trinity. Many of the pagan tenets, invented by the Egyptians and idealized by Plato, were retained as being worthy of belief."[55]

Dualism, as was popular in Gnosticism, held that spirit was good, and matter was evil. They were even said to have been created by different deities. Gnostics believed that the immortal soul was imprisoned in the body made of evil matter and longed to be freed. This Greek import causes many to exaggerate the conflict between the flesh and spirit as described by Paul. In extreme cases, any pleasure is seen as sinful, simply because it is pleasure; it gives pleasure to the flesh.

When the Creator made the world in six days, he saw that His creation was good. Then on the sixth day He put a single breeding pair of naked humans in the Garden, and behold it was *"very good."*[56] Flesh is not an evil substance which needs to be kept hidden for shame. Its desires must be kept within proper bounds and harnessed.

To a Hebraic mindset the conflict is between the *yetzer ha-tov* and the *yetzer ha-ra*, the inclination to good and the inclination to do bad, respectively. The two inclinations are not polar opposites. The bad inclination contains all the drives and desires. The good inclination cannot be rid of it but must harness its power for the

---

53. One God, *Plato*.
54. Strong, *Trinity*, 553.
55. Gibbon, *History*, 27.
56. Gen 1:31, emphasis added.

good. The two inclinations are seen as part of the design of the Creator and are there for a good purpose.

Perhaps the best description of the interplay of *yetzer ha-tov* and *yetzer ha-ra* in Jewish literature is in the Star trek episode, *The Enemy Within*. In a bizarre transporter accident, Captain Kirk is divided into his good and evil selves. Eventually, the two personalities figure out that they need to be reintegrated to be a single functioning individual. Neither could function without the other.

Filtering Hebraic literature through a Greek lens leads to doctrines and beliefs completely foreign to both the Hebrew scriptures and the Nazarean Writings commonly called the New Testament. These foreign doctrines have become so ingrained a habit in the Hellenized church, that even so much as asking questions about them can result in violent or *ad hominem* attacks.

The People of Israel, from ancient days were instructed to expect God's Annointed, a descendant of King David from the Tribe of Judah. There was never any suggestion by the prophets that this *Moshiach*, Messiah, would be anything other than a human like the rest of us. He is to be a prophet like Moses,[57] to come from among *Am Yisrael*, the People of Israel.

Simon Peter the Apostle describes Messiah as "a man approved of God."[58] Paul tells us that "There is one God, and one mediator between God and man, the man Christ Jesus."[59] He doesn't say "the God Christ Jesus," nor the "God-man," nor "God-the-Son," but simply "the man Christ Jesus."

Many scholars admit that the "deity of Christ" is never explicitly taught in either the Old Testament or the New, but is to be inferred.[60] James Dunn concludes, "The New Testament writers are really quite careful at this point. Jesus is not the God of Israel. He is not the Father. He is not Yahweh."[61] That a doctrine said to be so fundamental as to be virtually a condition of salvation is not

---

57. Deut 18:15, Acts 3:22, 7:37.
58. Acts 2:22.
59. 1 Tim 2:5.
60. Stanford, *History*.
61. Dunn, *Worship*, 142.

clearly set forth in Scripture, but can only be inferred, should give any lover of truth grave concern.

I suggest that the various Trinity theories, none of which is comprehensible to mortal humans, are not the best inference which may be drawn from Scriptural data. We will see below that the Hebrew concept of Agency provides a model which is not only imminently understandable, but better explains the data in a manner which does not require the equivocation and mental gymnastics that Trinity theory requires.

In his *An History of the Corruption of Christianity*,[62] Joseph Priestley traces the development of this and other doctrines from the teachings of Jesus and the Apostles, or "primitive Christianity," to what has come to be known as "orthodox Christianity."[63] He writes that the Greeks who dominated the proto-orthodox church perceived a need to improve on the reputation of a crucified messiah.

Dunn argues that identifying Jesus with God was an early attempt at resolving tensions which arose from the speculations of the church synods.[64] The authorized participants in these councils were heavily influenced by Hellenism, to the exclusion of Hebraic thought. It can be argued that the orthodoxy that emerged from various church councils, such as those at Nicaea and Chalcedon, is not so much a corruption of the original, but something entirely unrelated to the first century Nazarean Judaism taught and practiced by the first generation of believers. Historically, the councils produced creeds and dogmas well before the New Testament was canonized. The creeds, then were the final authority to which Scripture must be conformed, and not the other way around.

Those who disagreed with dogma, especially on the ground that it was contrary to the plain meaning of the sacred text, were

---

62. Priestley, *History*.

63. A distinction needs to be made between "orthodox Christianity," which is the set of doctrines generally accepted by most churches, and "Orthodox Christianity," which collectively refers to the churches of the Eastern branch of the great schism.

64. Dunn, *Worship*, 141.

exiled, burned as heretics or otherwise silenced. This continued through the Reformation, and to a lesser degree continues to this day. With the advent of the internet and other improvements in communication, it is more difficult to silence opposing voices.

In his Master's thesis,[65] Thomas Gaston traces the development of the doctrine of Trinity. It began as ideas imported from Platonist philosophy. Even by the end of the second century, the scope of his research, it had not taken the shape presently held as sacred by today's orthodox believers. Gaston's advantage in the study of the development of the doctrine lies in the fact that he is an historian, not a theologian; he has no doctrinal dog in the fight. The orthodox claim that "all true believers have always believed in the Trinity" is demonstrably unsupportable.

In his introduction, Gaston writes,

> In contemporary theology views on the origin of the doctrine of the Trinity range between two extremes: that the Trinity is explicit in the New Testament, on the one hand, and that the Trinity has no foundation in the Bible, on the other. A review of the tertiary literature demonstrates that the former position, though still represented by conservative theologians, is generally surrendered (in the face of historical considerations) for the middle position that the doctrine of the Trinity was implicit in the Scriptures and was made explicit by the developments of the Church Fathers. Historians have generally concluded that the doctrine of the Trinity was not original.

Anthony Hanson takes the issue ever farther:

> No responsible New Testament scholar would claim that the doctrine of the Trinity was taught by Jesus, or preached by the earliest Christians, or consciously held by any writer of the New Testament. It was in fact slowly worked out in the course of the first few centuries.[66]

History demonstrates that such fundamental doctrines as Trinity, immortality of the soul and immediate afterlife came into

65. Gaston, *Proto-Trinity*, 6.
66. Hanson, *Image*, 87.

Christian Drift

Christianity from Platonism, not from Scripture. When orthodox Christians defend what they call "sound doctrine," they are usually unaware that their doctrines are not original to the first century Jesus Movement but represent a departure from the Apostles' Doctrine. The official church councils claimed the authority to decree dogmas by asserting that:

> In the Old Testament God gave authority to the priests to interpret his laws and issue binding doctrine based on those interpretations, even with regard to criminal and civil issues – both through divine revelation (cf. Lev. 20:1–27, 25:1–55). In the New Testament, he endowed the Church with a charism to *teach infallibly*.[67]

William Wenstrom writes that while Yeshua's pre-existence is never stated in Scripture, it is "everywhere assumed." It is a necessary doctrine to support such fundamental doctrines as incarnation, hypostatic union, deity of Christ, and Trinity. He goes so far as to say, "If our Lord is not preexistent, He cannot be God, and if He is not God, He cannot be the Creator or Redeemer."[68]

He is correct; Yeshua's alleged pre-existence is nowhere supported by Scripture. It is not assumed anywhere in scripture, but is a mandatory belief, assumed to be true "everywhere" within orthodox Christendom. Wenstrom thus inadvertently admits that his entire Christian faith has no basis in the Bible. His other conclusions also naturally follow: there is no Trinity, Jesus is not God, and Jesus is not the Creator. These doctrines are the inventions of church councils and synods, decreed without an agreed upon New Testament canon. For over 1700 years, orthodox Christianity has been obliged to make Scripture conform to doctrine, rather than conforming their doctrines to the plain meaning of Scripture. Old habits die hard.

It is not permissible to demand that Scripture support a doctrine by implication, simply because that doctrine is necessary to support some other doctrine. Physicist Steven Weinberg wrote,

---

67. Sungenis, *Alone*, 315, emphasis added.
68. Wenstrom, *Revisited*, 1.

"Whatever the final laws of nature may be, there is no reason to suppose that they are designed to make physicists happy."[69] Neither is there any reason to suppose that the Bible was designed to make theologians happy.

We are not obligated to believe anything that is not spelled out in the Bible. Article VI of the Anglican Articles of Religion succinctly states this proposition in a manner with which most Protestants can agree:

> Holy Scriptures containeth all things necessary to salvation: so that whatsoever is not read therein, nor may be proved thereby, is not to be required of any man, that it should be believed as an article of the Faith, or be thought requisite or necessary to salvation.[70]

In violation of this precept, orthodox Christianity regularly requires adherents to subscribe to creedal statements which, as we have seen, are not explicitly set out in Holy Writ. Nor, as we have seen, are these extrabiblical creeds provable by principled examination of the text.

---

69. Weinberg, *Explain*, 90.
70. Suter, *Prayer*, 603.

Departures from Apostles' Doctrine

ONE BISHOP

New Testament narrative takes us from Yeshua's birth to just before the destruction of the Temple ca 70CE.[1] Little documentation from 70 to 100CE survives.

When written history revives in about 100CE, Ignatius of Antioch becomes the first bishop to act like a bishop. He decreed that there should be one bishop, rather than a committee of elders, as a protection against heresy. Aside from being unscriptural in itself, it was too late. Much error had already infiltrated the church, and the concentration of power served to cast error in concrete. The divinely designed protection against heresy was that the disciples should study the scriptures, in part as a check against elders going astray. This worked better in Jewish assemblies, since there has always been a high degree of literacy among Jews. The Greeks, except for a relatively wealthy few, did not generally learn to read. Eventually, the "laity" were forbidden to possess or read their Bibles for over a thousand years until the Protestant Reformation.

Ignatius was the first to insist that elders of formerly autonomous local assemblies be subject to his authority. He also decreed that no Eucharist could be held without at least a bishop presiding.

---

1. Bullinger, *Companion*, appendix 180.

UNIFORMITY OF DOCTRINE

As Greek speaking Gentiles began to dominate the Movement, they imported their Platonist philosophy, and tried to explain a Jewish Messiah in Hellenistic terms. Much was lost in the translation.

Among the earliest major blunders of the Church as it "moved . . . further from Mount Sinai and closer to Mars Hill,"[2] was the notion that all doctrine should be uniform, and that questions of right belief should be settled in synods, councils and conventions. This may well be among the last errors corrected in any reformation movement.

Typically, when a new Christian organization, whether a congregation, a denomination, or a parachurch ministry, is formed, the first order of business is to adopt a "statement of beliefs," a set of "articles of faith." These beliefs and articles will usually be precisely those which members brought from their previous organizations, unchanged and unexamined.

Judaism, on the other hand has always functioned, and still functions, without unanimity. It is inherent in the Talmudic method that *talmidim*, life-long learners of Torah, will disagree with one another. The saying "where there are two Jews, there will be three opinions" refers to this method. Two of the opinions will be the ones held before they begin, the third is the product of their discussions.

Their arguments might even become heated. This is acceptable, as long as it is an "argument for the sake of Heaven," that is, as long as the motive is to uncover truth. Both sides come out ahead in an argument for the sake of Heaven. The third opinion is likely to bring the debaters closer to the truth.

Early church councils, on the other hand, were characterized by venom and vituperation. Opponents called each other "enemies of Christ." Bishops advocated their positions in order to prevail and have their opinions become the official dogma. Winners anathematized and excommunicated the losers. Losers were exiled. This is an "argument *not* for the sake of Heaven." The victorious faction

---

2. Wilson, *Abraham*, 90.

Departures from Apostles' Doctrine

is likely to be farther from truth than before. Truth can stand on its own; error requires violence for its enforcement.

And what sort of questions brought all this rancor? Did the Holy Spirit proceed (whatever that means) from the Father alone? Or from the Father *and* the Son? Or from the Father *through* the Son?

The advantage to mandatory creeds is that they tend to keep doctrine from changing too quickly. Unfortunately, there is no guarantee that human-composed creeds are biblically accurate. And once the bishops make their decree, all further development ceases. No more discussion is allowed.

Meyers writes:

> Our obsessions with right worship and right belief may sound noble. It might even be mistaken for deep faith, but it is ultimately a form of individual and institutional narcissism. It promises an end to uncertainty, ambiguity, even mystery. But doubt is a precondition of faith, not its antithesis.[3]

Another hazard is that one who can recite a creed may be lulled into a false sense of security, thinking that the creed contains all he needs to know. The Dunning-Kruger Effect, in a nutshell, describes how it is that people who know nothing think that they know everything. Overly simplified, someone who has a half-pint of knowledge, expertise or competence in a particular subject matter can perceive that there may be a couple of teaspoonfuls of information still beyond his possession. Thus, he will overestimate his abilities in that area. One with a gallon of expertise recognizes that there is a barrel that he doesn't have. One with a barrel of competence knows that there is an ocean waiting to be explored.[4]

The Effect explains recent phenomena such as a famous teenager who thinks she knows everything there is to know about climate change, even surpassing PhDs in the field, or atheists on social media who have never read the New Testament who purport

---

3. Meyers, *Spiritual*, 45.
4. Psychology Today, *Dunning*.

to answer the question, "What Would Jesus Do?" better than life-long bible scholars. People who have extremely limited knowledge simply don't know that they don't know.

Thinking Hebraically, the Hebrews have not generally been interested in the questions which Christians have been wrestling with for centuries: What is the nature of the Godhead? To an Israelite the *Shema* is enough: "Listen Israel, YHVH [is] our God, YHVH [is] one." Who needs more than that? What is important is how to live this life in this world. And what is a "Godhead," anyway? The nature of Messiah was never in question in Hebrew thought. He would be a man, a prophet like Moses from among his brethren. There was never a perceived need for Messiah to be any kind of "divine being." That idea came from Plato, not Moses.

Judaism has never seen a need for uniformity of doctrine, which the Hellenized Church considers indispensable. Arguing out differences of opinion is how knowledge increases. Where there are mandatory creeds and fundamental doctrines, discussion ceases and learning with it.

ONE GOD

In about 110CE, Justin Martyr is credited with being the first church father to explicitly call Jesus "God." In Justin's description, Jesus as God was not on a par with the Father, who was the God of Israel, but a "second God" inferior and subordinate to the Father.

In the late second century or early third, Tertullian coined the term "*trinitas*," commonly rendered in English as trinity. At the time *trinitas* meant a triad, three of something. Later theologians' allegation that "trinity" is a contraction of "tri-unity" is anachronistic. It would be yet another 150 to 200 years before a church council would, by majority vote, decree that a Christian must believe that there are three persons in one Godhead. Tertullian's *trinitas* would retroactively become a heresy.

Third century theologian Origen originated terms like "hypostasis" and "eternal generation." In his view, only the Father was

Departures from Apostles' Doctrine

uncreated. The Son was the creation of the Father and the Holy Spirit was created by the Father through the Son.

Not until the Council of Nicaea in 325 was the Son declared to be just as much God as the Father is God. The Holy Spirit was voted to be co-equal God with the Father and Son at the Council of Constantinople in 381. This was the first time that official Church dogma held that the "Godhead" consisted eternally in three co-equal, co-eternal "Persons." Justin's subordinationism, which was "orthodox" when he propounded it, now became "heresy." Not until the middle of the fourth century did a majority of Christians believe in Jesus' alleged pre-existence. [5]

Long before the bishops began to debate the identity of Messiah and the nature of God, Plato, *circa* 360 BCE, had a trinity that consisted of the *Agathon*, the Supreme Good; the *Logos* or *Nous*, Reason, Mind, Intellect; and *Psuche*, soul. They were thought of as separate *hypostases*, or natures. The second emanated from the first, and the third was produced by the first and second, yet there was never a time when all three were not present. The *Agathon* was thought to be too transcendent to have any personal interaction with the material world. The *Agathon*, therefore created the material world through the *Logos*. The *Psuche* was the invisible divine power at work in the world. They were seen as three gods, yet comprising one *theion*, one divinity.[6]

Parallel to the development of Trinity speculation, a canon of Scripture was forming. The Masoretic text of the Hebrew Scriptures came to be authoritative in Rabbinic Judaism. But there is nothing surviving from the Masoretes older than the 9th century CE. There are differences between the Masoretic text and the Septuagint, the Greek translation, dating from the 3rd or 4th century BCE. The Pharisees recognize the Masoretic text of the *Tanakh*, but the Saducees and Samaritans recognize only the Pentateuch, the five books of Moses. As late as the Academy at Yavne, there was debate among the Rabbis as to whether Esther should be included,

---

5. Davis, *Development*.
6. Ware, *Outline*, 9–12.

since God is never mentioned by name, and whether to include Song of Songs, because it is too racy to read publicly.

Similarly, several church fathers proposed their own lists of authoritative writings. Any given bishop's list was authoritative only within his diocese. The New Testament canon was not approved by a vote until at least the Synod of Hippo in 393 under the auspices of Augustine. During the Protestant Reformation, each protesting sect made its own decisions as to what writings were authoritative Scripture. For Roman Catholicism, the Council of Trent in 1546 re-ratified its canon in response to the Protestants.

Thus, by 381CE, the bishops had entirely purged the Hebraic idea of the indivisible unity of the Creator and replaced it with Platonist philosophical speculation, all without an agreed text of New Testament writings.

Passages altered to support Trinity

It is well known among scholars that scribes have not always copied the Scriptures faithfully. Usually, variants occur innocently through human error. Sometimes, changes are made deliberately. The scribe tries to amend the text for clarity, or to support a particular doctrine. Here are a few well-known changes from the original.

The "Johannine Comma"

1 John 5:7-8 in the King James Version reads:

> For there are three that bear record in heaven, the Father, the Word, and the Holy Ghost: and these three are one. And there are three that bear witness in earth, the Spirit, and the water, and the blood: and these three agree in one.

This passage is the only on-point verse with "three-in-one" language in the entire Protestant canon. However, the same passage in the NIV is:

Departures from Apostles' Doctrine

> For there are three that testify: the Spirit, the water and the blood; and the three are in agreement.

Most modern versions agree with the NIV. Some older translations, like the KJV, have the controversial verse. Why is there disagreement among the versions about including "three that bear record in heaven, the Father, the Word, and the Holy Ghost?" Why do some versions have that verse and others do not? This passage is controversial enough to have a name. It is called the "Johannine Comma."

It first appears in Latin *circa* 545CE and does not appear in a Greek New Testament until Erasmus' third edition *circa* 1522.[7] Scholars almost universally recognize it as inauthentic.[8]

There is an oft told, but probably unhistorical story about Desiderius Erasmus who published the first critical Greek New Testament after the invention of the printing press. It is said that he omitted the only explicit proof text for the Trinity because it was not in any Greek text available to him. This much is historical. The less probable part of the story is that when he was called on the carpet for leaving it out, the bishop accused him of deliberately omitting this important passage to disparage the Doctrine of the Trinity. He explained that he left it out, simply because it was not in a manuscript available to him, He promised to include it in future editions if the bishop could produce a manuscript containing the verse. So, the bishop commissioned one to be written, back-translating from the Vulgate.

While plausible, more recent scholarship casts doubt on the story. What remains is that Erasmus' first two editions do not contain the contested verse. It was added to his third and subsequent editions. It is also well known that some copyists have been known to amend the text in order to make it seem to say what the copyist thought it ought to say. This illustrates the importance of textual research.

---

7. Erasmus. *New Testament*.
8. Marlowe. *Comma*.

Some scholars say that the Comma first appeared in a marginal note in Jerome's Latin Vulgate. The edition of the Vulgate which appears in www.blueletterbible.org does not contain the verse.

The Mystery of Godliness

In the King James Version, 1 Timothy 3:16 reads: "And without controversy great is the mystery of godliness: God was manifest in the flesh, justified in the Spirit, seen of angels, preached unto the Gentiles, believed on in the world, received up into glory." This verse is commonly cited by trinitarians to support their doctrine. Most English versions do not read the same. Of the 60 versions listed at biblegateway.com, only 16 read " . . . God was manifested . . . " 31 English versions read, " . . . he was . . . " Seven have some other third person singular pronoun. Four versions read Jesus or Christ was manifested. There are also paraphrases, where the translators' opinion superseded the text.

Why the difference? Why do some versions read "God," and some say "he?" The difference is in variants of the Greek text. Some manuscripts have ΘΕΟΣ, *Theos* or God, and some have 'ΟΣ, *hos*, which or 'Ο, *ho*, who.

Which variant is correct? The oldest manuscripts have 'ΟΣ, *hos*, which or 'Ο, *ho*, who. ΘΕΟΣ, *Theos* does not appear until after church councils had decreed trinitarian doctrine in the late fourth century. Some of the oldest have an abbreviation for Theos $\overline{\Theta\Sigma}$ with an overscore to indicate an abbreviation. It is easy to see that it would take no extraordinary effort to change "which" into an abbreviation for "God."

Since Greek verbs do not need a subject pronoun, "which" is a more likely translation than "he." "He" is included in the conjugation of the verb.

A more accurate rendering of the verse would be, "And without controversy great is the mystery of godliness, *which* was manifest in the flesh, justified in the Spirit, seen of angels, preached unto the Gentiles, believed on in the world, received up into glory." Godliness was manifested, not God.

The days are probably past when a mischievous scribe can slip changes into the original language copies of Scripture. There is simply too much well-known information accessible to even the most casual of students. Still, much mischief occurs in translation. Sometimes it is innocent, sometimes it is deliberate.

Not so innocent are the changes some versions make. Rather than impute nefarious intent, we presume that such emendations are good faith efforts to explain the text for the reader, in the light of the translator's presuppositions.

For example:

- (NiRV) There is no doubt that godliness is a great mystery. Jesus appeared in a body.
- (NLT) Without question, this is the great mystery of our faith: Christ was revealed in a human body and vindicated by the Spirit.
- (WNT) And, beyond controversy, great is the mystery of our religion-- that Christ appeared in human form, and His claims justified by the Spirit.

No Greek text to my knowledge has "Jesus" or "Christ" in this verse. The translators either innocently meant to explain things to the reader, or deliberately altered the text in translation to make the Scripture say what the translator thought it ought to say. In either event, such emendations mislead the reader.

Re-Examining Misconstrued Passages in Light of Hebrew Reasoning

WE ALL COME TO the text of Scripture with our own set of cultural lenses. To recover the meaning of Scripture as intended by those who wrote it, we must set aside 1900 years of Hellenistic habit and acquire a Hebraic mental lens. Old habits die hard. It may be difficult to make this change. But if we re-examine traditional interpretations from a Hebrew point of view, we will see that many passages do not mean what we were taught that they mean.

AGENCY

Just as the importance of the Jewishness of the original Nazarean movement cannot be overemphasized, the principle of Agency in Jewish law must be recognized. Failure to recognize Agency has resulted in serious theological confusion. Agency law survives in secular law, as well.

"An agent is a person authorized by another to act for him, one entrusted (*sic*) with another's business."[1] Actors hire agents to negotiate contracts for parts in plays or films. A patient might give an agent a health care power of attorney. An attorney-in-fact, the agent named in a power of attorney, does not need to be a licensed

---

1. Black, *Dictionary*, "Agent."

attorney-at-law. An agent can be appointed either informally by oral agreement, or by written formalities. Though in some matters, a writing is necessary.

James McGrath tells us, "*Agency was an important part of every day life in the ancient world. Individuals such as prophets and angels mentioned in the Jewish Scriptures were thought of as "agents" of God.* And the key idea regarding agency in the ancient world appears to be summarized in the phrase from rabbinic literature so often quoted in these contexts: "*The one sent is like the one who sent him.*"[2]

The agent is called *shaliach* in Hebrew, a "sent one" from *shalach*, send. God instructed Moses to send, *shalach*, twelve scouts to "Spy out" the Promised Land.[3] The Septuagint uses *apostolos*, apostle, to translate *shaliach* into Greek. One day, Yeshua gathered his disciples and chose twelve, whom he appointed as apostles,[4] *shaliachim*, agents to do his business in his name.

Examples of agency abound in Scripture.

- In Genesis 24 Abraham sends his servant back to the old country to negotiate for a wife for Isaac.[5]

- In Genesis 38, Judah whose wife had died sought solace from his daughter-in-law Tamar, mistaking her for a prostitute. He left his signet, bracelets, and staff as collateral against the price they agreed on. He later sent his friend Hira the Abdullamite with the agreed-on fee to act on his behalf to recover the collateral.

- Joseph was appointed as Pharaoh's agent over all Egypt. Pharaoh said to him, "Thou shalt be over my house, and

2. McGrath, *Only*, 14, emphasis added.
3. Num 13:1–20.
4. Luke 6:13.
5. The servant is not identified by name, but many suppose that the expedition was led by Eleazar, Abraham's chief of staff. There were most likely others in the entourage, as no one would travel alone through wilderness in those days, especially carrying the assets described. Brigands and highwaymen abounded.

according unto thy word shall all my people be ruled: only in the throne will I be greater than thou."

- Moses was God's agent to bring the Israelites out of Egypt.

It is important to realize that "a person's agent is regarded as the person himself. Therefore, any act committed by a duly appointed agent is regarded as having been committed by the principal."[6] This is the basis of holding an employer liable for the wrongs committed by an employee while in the course of his employment, as is still the secular law today.[7]

This principle is illustrated by the two descriptions of the centurion asking Yeshua for healing for his sick employee. Matthew[8] reports the conversation as though Yeshua and the centurion were speaking face to face. Luke[9] reports the conversation taking place through intermediaries. The centurion sent (*apostello, shalach*) emissaries saying " . . . I am not worthy that thou shouldest enter under my roof: Wherefore neither thought I myself worthy to come unto thee . . . "[10]

The thoroughly Jewish audience to whom these Gospels were written would have recognized the principle of agency involved. They would see that there is no contradiction between the two accounts. Matthew simply left out the detail of intermediaries as not necessary to the story. When the agents acted for the centurion; it is as though the centurion acted in person. The messengers need not be noticed any more than an interpreter translating a conversation between two people who have no common language between them.

When God and Moses have a conversation at the burning bush, the "Angel of the Lord" acts as Yehovah's agent:

> Now Moses kept the flock of Jethro his father in law, the priest of Midian: and he led the flock to the backside of

6. One, *Agency*.
7. Black, *Dictionary*, "Respondeat superior."
8. Matt 8:6–10.
9. Luke 7:2–10.
10. Luke 7:6–7.

the desert, and came to the mountain of God, even to Horeb.

And the angel of the LORD appeared unto him in a flame of fire out of the midst of a bush: and he looked, and, behold, the bush burned with fire, and the bush was not consumed.

And Moses said, I will now turn aside, and see this great sight, why the bush is not burnt.

And when the LORD saw that he turned aside to see, God called unto him out of the midst of the bush, and said, Moses, Moses. And he said, Here am I.

And he said, Draw not nigh hither: put off thy shoes from off thy feet, for the place whereon thou standest is holy ground.

Moreover he said, I am the God of thy father, the God of Abraham, the God of Isaac, and the God of Jacob. And Moses hid his face; for he was afraid to look upon God.

And the LORD said, I have surely seen the affliction of my people which are in Egypt, and have heard their cry by reason of their taskmasters; for I know their sorrows;

And I am come down to deliver them out of the hand of the Egyptians, and to bring them up out of that land unto a good land and a large, unto a land flowing with milk and honey; unto the place of the Canaanites, and the Hittites, and the Amorites, and the Perizzites, and the Hivites, and the Jebusites.

Now therefore, behold, the cry of the children of Israel is come unto me: and I have also seen the oppression wherewith the Egyptians oppress them.

Come now therefore, and I will send thee unto Pharaoh, that thou mayest bring forth my people the children of Israel out of Egypt.

And Moses said unto God, Who am I, that I should go unto Pharaoh, and that I should bring forth the children of Israel out of Egypt?

And he said, Certainly I will be with thee; and this shall be a token unto thee, that I have sent thee: When thou hast brought forth the people out of Egypt, ye shall serve God upon this mountain.

Notice that the "Angel of Yehovah" appeared, but the conversation is reported, as "Yehovah said," "God called." Some would manufacture a contradiction here, but if we take into account the principle of agency, there is no contradiction. A Hebrew mind would see the angel acting as *shaliach*, bearing his principal's name and title. A western, literal mind sees God's side of the conversation coming from two distinct entities.

Some claim that the angel is Jesus in his alleged pre-existence.[11] But as van Noort points out, "Jesus wasn't an angel, nor was an angel ever a son."[12] He cites Hebrews 1:5, "For to which of the angels did He ever say, 'You are my son?'" Nor is there any verse which supports the idea that Jesus "pre-existed" himself. As Matthew clearly tells us, Yeshua's beginning was at his conception.[13]

There are many verses which clearly distinguish Jesus from God. The Father is the only true God.[14] The Father is greater than I.[15] No one knows the time [of the end], not the angels nor the Son but the Father only.[16] Of myself I can do nothing . . . I only do what the Father shows me.[17] My God, my God Why have you forsaken me?[18] The birth (*genesis*, beginning) of Jesus Christ was in this manner.[19] He is called the Son of God,[20] never "God the Son."

---

11. Mamatha, *Jesus*.
12. Van Noort, *Who*, 528.
13. Matt 1:18.
14. John 17:3.
15. John 14:28.
16. Mark 13:32.
17. John 5:19, 30.
18. Matt 27:46, Mark 15:34, Ps 22:1.
19. Matt 1:18 Greek *genesis*, origin or beginning. Some MSS read *gennesis*, birth. The extra *Nu* or N seems to be a later interpolation.
20. Luke 1:35.

Re-Examining Misconstrued Passages in Light of Hebrew Reasoning

There are also verses which are mustered to suggest that Jesus is, in fact God. I and my Father are one.[21] Before Abraham was, I am.[22] The Word was made flesh and dwelt among us.[23] And so on.

The apparent tension between these two sets of passages needs resolution, in accordance with the principle of non-contradiction. Pro-deity advocates explain the non-deity verses with post-biblical doctrines, such as dual nature and hypostatic union. Pro-humanity advocates explain the apparent deity passages with principles like the Jewish concept of agency, and by correcting mistranslations. In any translation, the translator must make choices about which of several ways a word or phrase could be rendered. The choices made will inevitably be colored by the translators' opinions and presuppositions.

Yeshua describes himself in terms of agency for his Father, the only true God:

- Mat 10:40 - He that receiveth you receiveth me, and he that receiveth me receiveth him that sent me.

- Mar 9:37 - Whosoever shall receive one of such children in my name, receiveth me: and whosoever shall receive me, receiveth not me, but him that sent me.

- Luke 4:18 - The Spirit of the Lord is upon me, because he hath anointed me to preach the gospel to the poor; he hath sent me to heal the brokenhearted, to preach deliverance to the captives, and recovering of sight to the blind, to set at liberty them that are bruised (Quoting Isa 61:1).

- Luke 9:48 - And said unto them, Whosoever shall receive this child in my name receiveth me: and whosoever shall receive me receiveth him that sent me: for he that is least among you all, the same shall be great.

- John 4:34 - Jesus saith unto them, My meat is to do the will of him that sent me, and to finish his work.

21. John 10:30.
22. John 8:58.
23. John 1:14.

- John 5:24 - Verily, verily, I say unto you, He that heareth my word, and believeth on him that sent me, hath everlasting life, and shall not come into condemnation; but is passed from death unto life.

- John 5:30 - I can of mine own self do nothing: as I hear, I judge: and my judgment is just; because I seek not mine own will, but the will of the Father which hath sent me.

- John 5:36 - But I have greater witness than that of John: for the works which the Father hath given me to finish, the same works that I do, bear witness of me, that the Father hath sent me.

- John 5:37 - And the Father himself, which hath sent me, hath borne witness of me. Ye have neither heard his voice at any time, nor seen his shape.

- John 6:38 - For I came down from heaven, not to do mine own will, but the will of him that sent me.[24]

- John 6:39 - And this is the Father's will which hath sent me, that of all which he hath given me I should lose nothing, but should raise it up again at the last day.

- John 15:9 - As the Father hath loved me, so have I loved you: continue ye in my love

He also describes his followers as his agents:

- Matt 10:40 - He that receiveth you receiveth me, and he that receiveth me receiveth him that sent me.

- Luke 10:16 - He that heareth you heareth me; and he that despiseth you despiseth me; and he that despiseth me despiseth him that sent me.

---

24. "I have come down from heaven." Jesus said that he came from heaven, meaning that He came from God; God was his source. The Jews would not have taken Christ's words to mean that he "incarnated" or was somehow God. It was a common use of language for them to say that something "came from heaven" if God were its source, and there are a number of verses that show that is true. Spirit and Truth, *Revised*, footnote at John 6:38.

Re-Examining Misconstrued Passages in Light of Hebrew Reasoning

- John 15:18 - If the world hate you, ye know that it hated me before it hated you.

Yeshua says that when someone persecutes his disciples, he himself is being persecuted:

> And Saul, yet breathing out threatenings and slaughter against the disciples of the Lord, went unto the high priest, And desired of him letters to Damascus to the synagogues, that if he found any of this way, whether they were men or women, he might bring them bound unto Jerusalem. And as he journeyed, he came near Damascus: and suddenly there shined round about him a light from heaven:
> And he fell to the earth, and heard a voice saying unto him, Saul, Saul, why persecutest thou me? And he said, Who art thou, Lord? And the Lord said, I am Jesus whom thou persecutest:[25]

He tells Saul that in persecuting Jesus' disciples, he is persecuting Jesus. His disciples are his agents, just as he is God's agent.

When an agent, a *shaliach* acts, it is as though the principle himself is acting. Thus, Yeshua could say, I and my Father are one.[26] If you have seen me, you have seen the Father.[27] This is a claim of agency, not divinity. He prays to his Father, the only true God,[28] that his disciples would "be one, as we *are*."[29] If being one with God means *being* God, then being one with each other, as he prayed, means that we *are* each other. This violates the principle of avoiding absurd conclusions. As *shaliach*, the angel can tell Moses from the burning bush "I am the God of thy father, the God of Abraham, the God of Isaac, and the God of Jacob." A heavenly messenger saying "I am God" is not claiming to *be* God, but stating his status as agent on *behalf* of God.

---

25. Acts 9:1–5.
26. John 10:30.
27. John 14:9.
28. John 17:3.
29. John 17:11.

MY LORD AND MY GOD

The title "god" can be applied, in certain contexts, to other persons or entities than the One God of Israel. The rabbinic dictum that the "one sent is like the one who sent him" puts the agent in the place of the principal. Therefore the agent can be described in "divine language" and "sit on God's throne"[30]

Had Justin Martyr been aware of the Jewish principle of agency, he would not have needed to invent a "second god," subordinate to the transcendent Father. He would have realized, as did the first generation of Nazareans that the Son is an agent of the Father, who is the only true God. As agent, the Son may sit in the Father's throne, be "depicted in divine language," and "even bear the divine name."

Recall the Parable of the Vineyard:

> Hear another parable: There was a certain householder, which planted a vineyard, and hedged it round about, and digged a winepress in it, and built a tower, and let[31] it out to husbandmen, and went into a far country:
>
> And when the time of the fruit drew near, he sent his servants to the husbandmen, that they might receive the fruits of it.
>
> And the husbandmen took his servants, and beat one, and killed another, and stoned another.
>
> Again, he sent other servants more than the first: and they did unto them likewise.
>
> But last of all he sent unto them his son, saying, They will reverence my son.
>
> But when the husbandmen saw the son, they said among themselves, This is the heir; come, let us kill him, and let us seize on his inheritance.
>
> And they caught him, and cast him out of the vineyard, and slew him.
>
> When the lord therefore of the vineyard cometh, what will he do unto those husbandmen?

---

30. McGrath, *Only*, 14.
31. "Let" is the archaic verb form of "Lease."

> They say unto him, He will miserably destroy those wicked men, and will let out his vineyard unto other husbandmen, which shall render him the fruits in their seasons. [32]

The landlord let out his vineyard to tenants. When he sent agents acting in his behalf to collect the rent, the tenants abused the agents. This is the same as abusing the landlord. The landlord then sent his son as agent. A son, especially a firstborn, is the ideal agent. He looks like his father and is expected to inherit the family business one day.

When the Son acts for his Father, it is as though the Father Himself were acting.

While on the one hand, "I, *even* I, *am* the LORD; and beside me *there is* no saviour (Heb *yasha*, savior or deliverer),"[33] other people are referred to as *yasha*:

- Jdg 3:9 - And when the children of Israel cried unto the LORD, the LORD raised up a *deliverer* to the children of Israel, who delivered them, even *Othniel the son of Kenaz*, Caleb's younger brother.

- Jdg 3:15 - But when the children of Israel cried unto the LORD, the LORD raised them up a *deliverer, Ehud the son of Gera*, a Benjamite, a man lefthanded: and by him the children of Israel sent a present unto Eglon the king of Moab.

- Act 7:35 - This *Moses* whom they refused, saying, Who made thee a ruler and a judge? The same did God send to be a ruler and a *deliverer* by the hand of the angel which appeared to him in the bush.

- Rom 11:26 - And so all Israel shall be saved: as it is written, There shall come out of Sion the *Deliverer*, and shall turn away ungodliness from Jacob:

---

32. Matt 21:33–41, also see Luke 20:9–16.
33. Isa 43:11.

When Yehovah delivers His people through human agents, the agents are called "savior" or "deliverer," but God alone is the ultimate source of deliverance.

- 2Sa 22:2 - And he said, The Lord is my rock, and my fortress, and my deliverer.
- Psa 18:2 - The Lord is my rock, and my fortress, and my deliverer; my God, my strength, in whom I will trust; my buckler, and the horn of my salvation, and my high tower.
- Psa 40:17 - But I am poor and needy; yet the Lord thinketh upon me: thou art my help and my deliverer; make no tarrying, O my God.
- Psa 70:5 - But I am poor and needy: make haste unto me, O God: thou art my help and my deliverer; O Lord, make no tarrying.
- Psa 144:2 - My goodness, and my fortress; my high tower, and my deliverer; my shield, and he in whom I trust; who subdueth my people under me.

Human rulers are also called "gods." When an indentured servant is due to be releases, but chooses to stay with his master,

> And if the servant shall plainly say, I love my master, my wife, and my children; I will not go out free: Then his master shall bring him unto the judges (Heb *elohim* "gods"); he shall also bring him to the door, or unto the door post; and his master shall bore his ear through with an aul; and he shall serve him for ever.[34]

And,

> If a man shall deliver unto his neighbour money or stuff to keep, and it be stolen out of the man's house; if the thief be found, let him pay double.
> If the thief be not found, then the master of the house shall be brought unto the judges (*elohim*), to see whether he have put his hand unto his neighbour's goods.

---

34. Exod 21:5–6.

> For all manner of trespass, whether it be for ox, for ass, for sheep, for raiment, or for any manner of lost thing, which another challengeth to be his, the cause of both parties shall come before the judges; and whom the judges (*elohim*) shall condemn, he shall pay double unto his neighbour.[35]

Angels are also called "gods."

> What is man, that thou art mindful of him? and the son of man, that thou visitest him? For thou hast made him a little lower than the angels (*elohim*), and hast crowned him with glory and honour.[36]

When King Saul consults a medium, the medium is frightened and says, "I saw gods (*elohim*) coming up out of the earth."[37] Whatever these spirits might have been, they were not the Creator.

Human rulers are not literally gods. As God's agents in dispensing justice they stand in God's place and share in the title. Angels are not gods. As God's agents delivering messages[38] they speak in God's name, and thus stand in His place.

When Yeshua's enemies (!) *mis*interpret his teaching and *erroneously* accuse him of "making himself God,"[39] he corrects them with an example from Scripture of the title of "god" applied to humans in the sense of agency:

> Jesus answered them, I told you, and ye believed not: *the works that I do in my Father's name,* they bear witness of me. But ye believe not, because ye are not of my sheep, as I said unto you. My sheep hear my voice, and I know them, and they follow me: And I give unto them eternal life; and they shall never perish, neither shall any man pluck them out of my hand. My Father, which gave them

---

35. Exod 22:7–9.
36. Ps 8:4–5.
37. 1 Sam 28:13.
38. The words translated as "angel," *malach* in Hebrew, and *aggellos* in Greek, both primarily mean "messenger."
39. John 10:33.

> me, is greater than all; and no man is able to pluck them out of my Father's hand.
> *I and my Father are one.*
> Then the Jews took up stones again to stone him.
> Jesus answered them, Many good works have I shewed you from my Father; for which of those works do ye stone me?
> The Jews answered him, saying, For a good work we stone thee not; but for blasphemy; and because that thou, being a man, makest thyself God.
> Jesus answered them, Is it not written in your law, I said, *Ye are gods?*[40] If he called them gods, unto whom the word of God came, and the scripture cannot be broken; Say ye of him, whom the Father hath sanctified, and sent into the world, Thou blasphemest; because I said, I am the Son of God?
> If I do not the works of my Father, believe me not.
> But if I do, though ye believe not me, believe the works: that ye may know, and believe, that the Father is in me, and I in him.[41]

Plainly, Yeshua was not claiming to *be* Yehovah, but claimed to be His *agent*, doing his "works" in the Father's name. "I and my Father are one" is not a claim to *be* the Father, but a statement of unity, not of essence, but of purpose.

When Thomas exclaims, "My Lord and my God," as a Jew, he was recognizing that his resurrected teacher was King Messiah, the man who mediated a renewal of the Covenant between God and humanity, in the name of God,[42] and not as God, Himself.

WORD MADE FLESH

John, the latest of the New Testament writers, begins his Gospel with the familiar passage:

---

40. Quoting Ps 82:6 "I have said, Ye are gods; and all of you are children of the Most High."
41. John 10:25–38, emphasis added.
42. 1 Tim 2:5.

Re-Examining Misconstrued Passages in Light of Hebrew Reasoning

> In the beginning was the Word, and the Word was with God, and the Word was God. The same was in the beginning with God. All things were made by him; and without him was not any thing made that was made . . . . And the word was made flesh and dwelt among us . . . [43]

Many Christians read this as though it says:

> In the beginning was Jesus, and Jesus was with God and Jesus was God. Jesus was in the beginning with God. All things were made by Jesus and without Jesus was not any thing made that was made. . . . And Jesus became flesh and dwelt among us.

While this alternate reading is consistent with mainstream dogma, that is not what is actually written.

How would a first century Jewish audience understand "all things were made by the Word," or "the Word was made flesh?" The opening of the *P'suchei d'Zimra*, the warmup section of a Jewish prayer service is "Blessed is he who only spake and the world existed! Blessed is he. Blessed is the Author of the creation. Blessed is he who sayeth and performeth."[44] The prayer service gelled some time after the Nazarean and Pharisee traditions diverged, but this passage reflects an earlier time, from the beginning of the Rabbinic era before the Nazarean movement began.

"By the word of the LORD were the heavens made and all the host of them by the breath of his mouth."[45] In the six days of the making of the heavens and the earth, God says, "Let there be . . . ." and it happens.

The word of the LORD is the words spoken by Yehovah. Philo personifies the Logos, much in the same way as Proverbs chapter 8 personifies Lady Wisdom.[46] In neither case is wisdom or *logos* to be understood as an actual person. They are examples of the figure of speech *personification*, where something inanimate is portrayed

---

43. John 1:1–3, 14.
44. Mendes, *Prayers*, 19.
45. Ps 33:6.
46. Davis, *Logos*.

as if it were a sentient being. But a personification is not literally a person.

Philo calls the Logos God's firstborn, in the sense that words are begotten or born when they are uttered. God spoke words and by these spoken words created the heavens and earth. It is anachronistic to retroactively impose fourth century Nicene thought on a first century Jewish writer.

"The LORD by wisdom hath founded the earth, by understanding hath he established the heavens."[47] "Wisdom" and "understanding" are not other entities; they are attributes of the Creator. Wisdom personified was "set up" and "brought forth"[48] before the earth was created. In an appropriate context, wisdom, understanding, torah, logos, *nomos, memra,* word, *devar*, are all rough synonyms for the words which proceed from God's mouth.

Torah, in its narrowest sense consists of the five books of Moses: Genesis, Exodus, Leviticus, Numbers, and Deuteronomy. In its broadest sense, it is all knowledge and truth; it is God's blueprint of the universe. Early western scientists, such as Locke, Newton, and Priestley, considered science to be "God's other book," after the Bible. The laws of physics are as much torah, in this sense, as the Torah is God's law. Astronomy is the Law, *nomos* of the stars, astro-nomia. Economics is the *nomos* of ordering a household, an *oikos*. Any scientific discipline ending in –ology is the *logos*, the instruction, of that discipline.

God's Word, whether expressed in revelation written by the prophets or in the laws of physics, is God's speech. Speech is not a separate entity from the speaker. In a criminal sentencing, the Judge might speak to the convicted defendant, saying, "It is the order, judgment and sentence of this Court that you be taken into the custody of the Sheriff of this county, to be transferred by him to the custody of the Secretary of Corrections, there to serve a term of not less than three years, nor more than ten years." He then bangs his gavel once, and the words he spoke happen. Such is the

47. Prov 3:19.
48. Prov 8:23–24.

power the word of an earthly judge. *Elohim* spoke and the world came to be; such is the power of the Word of the Heavenly Judge.

What, then, is the "Word made flesh," in a Jewish context? A parallel can be drawn to the Hasidic movement. Many disciples of a particularly saintly *rebbe* might see their rabbi as the embodiment of Torah. Since he is so dedicated to living by *halachah* that however he does things must be the Torah way of doing. The *Rebbe* will be considered the Torah made flesh. It is no exaggeration to say that they will even watch how he ties his shoes in the morning, then make and follow a law of shoe-tying.

> Rebbe Yochanan states that the left shoe should be put on first, since shoes are likened to tefillin which are tied on the left arm. Yet there is a baraita which states that the right shoe has precedence. The gemara concludes that we can fulfill both views by putting on the right first, according to the baraita, but respecting Rebbe Yochanan's view by tying the left first. The idea is that the likeness of shoes to tefillin is primarily in the aspect of tying; therefore, even according to Rebbe Yochanan the main importance is to tie the left first.[49]

In a manner similar to this, Paul tells his readers, "Be ye therefore followers (*mimetai*, imitatiors) of me, even as I also am of Christ."[50] When believers ask themselves rhetorically, "What Would Jesus Do?" it translates to "How should I act in imitation of the Living Torah/Logos in this situation?" John the Baptist pointed Yeshua out to two of his disciples as the "Lamb of God." And the two disciples heard him speak, and they followed Jesus.

> Then Jesus turned, and saw them following, and saith unto them, What seek ye? They said unto him, Rabbi, (which is to say, being interpreted, Master,) where dwellest thou?

---

49. Meir, *Wearing*.
50. 1 Cor 11:1.

He saith unto them, Come and see. They came and saw where he dwelt, and abode with him that day: for it was about the tenth hour.[51]

It is not too great a stretch to suggest that perhaps they wanted to see how he "tied his shoes," how he lived his life. By speech, the Creator created the heavens and the earth. That which was spoken is how the Messiah walked. We ought to walk as he walked,[52] which is according to the words which came from God's mouth, and thereby become, as much as flawed humans can, Logos made flesh, the Way, the Truth and the Life.

A favorite verse in Christendom is "Jesus saith unto him, I am the way, the truth, and the life: no man cometh unto the Father, but by me."[53] This is commonly understood to mean that those who make Jesus their lord go to heaven when they die and all others burn in Hell for all eternity, regardless of any mitigating circumstances, such as dying before the age of accountability. This may be a reasonable interpretation if one thinks like a Platonist Greek. I do not think that this is how the original Hebrew audience would understand it. Whatever its proper meaning, it cannot contradict the Psalmist who said, "The LORD is nigh unto all them that call upon him, to all that call upon him in truth."[54]

For the man who said, "I do nothing of myself . . . ,"[55] "My doctrine is not mine, but his that sent me,"[56] "The word which ye hear is not mine, but the Father which sent me,"[57] and "Take my yoke upon you, and learn of me; for I am meek and lowly in heart: and ye shall find rest unto your souls,"[58] it seems out of character to say (pardon the hyperbole) "*I* am the way, the truth, and the life:

---

51. John 1:37–39.
52. 1 John 2:6.
53. John 14:6.
54. Ps 145:18.
55. John 8:28.
56. John 7:16.
57. John 14:24.
58. Mat 11:29.

Re-Examining Misconstrued Passages in Light of Hebrew Reasoning

no man cometh unto the Father, but by *Meeee*" as many Christians seem to read it.

Let's look at the context:

> Let not your heart be troubled: ye believe in God, believe also in me. In my Father's house are many mansions: if it were not so, I would have told you. I go to prepare a place for you. And if I go and prepare a place for you, I will come again, and receive you unto myself; that where I am, there ye may be also. And whither I go ye know, and the way ye know.
>
> Thomas saith unto him, Lord, we know not whither thou goest; and how can we know the way?
>
> Jesus saith unto him, I am the way, the truth, and the life: no man cometh unto the Father, but by me. If ye had known me, ye should have known my Father also: and from henceforth ye know him, and have seen him.
>
> Philip saith unto him, Lord, shew us the Father, and it sufficeth us.
>
> Jesus saith unto him, Have I been so long time with you, and yet hast thou not known me, Philip? He that hath seen me hath seen the Father; and how sayest thou then, Shew us the Father? Believest thou not that I am in the Father, and the Father in me? The words that I speak unto you I speak not of myself: but the Father that dwelleth in me, he doeth the works.
>
> Believe me that I am in the Father, and the Father in me: or else believe me for the very works' sake. Verily, verily, I say unto you, He that believeth on me, the works that I do shall he do also; and greater works than these shall he do; because I go unto my Father. And whatsoever ye shall ask in my name, that will I do, that the Father may be glorified in the Son. If ye shall ask any thing in my name, I will do it.[59]

This passage is filled to overflowing with the principle of agency. From "you believe in God, believe also in me [His agent]," to "I am in the Father and the Father in me," Yeshua is explaining that he acts only in the Father's name. One who has *really* seen

---

59. John 14:1–14.

Yeshua has seen the Father because, while no one has seen God, the Son has made Him known.[60] Agency continues with, "He that believeth on me, the works that I do shall he do also; and greater works than these shall he do; because I go unto my Father." As Yeshua's agents, those who believe are granted authority to use his name to do the sort of things he did, just as the Father gave him authority[61] to use His name to do "mighty works."

Many orthodox Christians argue the Jesus must be God, because only God can work miracles. Here Yeshua says that his agents will do miraculous deeds in his name. Yeshua does nothing by himself but the Father in him does the work; Yeshua's agents can do nothing by themselves, but the Father in Yeshua in the agent does the work.

As Yehovah's chief agent, Yeshua is the path to the Father, Who is the only true God. "Way" in the way, the truth and the life, is *hodos* in Greek. *Hodos* means road, path, street and by extension journey, including life journey. Yeshua is our example how to walk according to the Creator's instruction as spelled out in Torah. Torah is our path, our way. We see then that Yeshua is called the *Logos* or *Torah* become flesh because he so lived the Word of God that by observing his manner or way of life, we can see what the Creator's instruction is. He so walked in the Father's way that he *is* the way.

The Word of God is truth.[62] The psalmist says, "Teach me thy way, O LORD; I will walk in thy truth: unite my heart to fear thy name."[63] God's way is truth. By observing the one who walks in truth, we can see what truth is.

The Word is life.[64] Yeshua said, "He that heareth my word, and believeth on him that sent me, hath everlasting life . . . "[65]

---

60. John 1:18.

61. Matt 28:18 And Jesus came and spake unto them, saying, All power is given unto me in heaven and in earth.

62. John 17:17, 1 Kgs 17:24.

63. Ps 86:11.

64. Phil 2:6, 1 John 1:1.

65. John 5:24.

Re-Examining Misconstrued Passages in Light of Hebrew Reasoning

To "believe" is not merely to accept a proposition as true. Believing implies action. The phrases above translated "believe in" or "believe on" are better translated "believe into." The preposition in both cases is the Greek word *eis*, not *en*. *Eis* describes motion toward and arriving at a destination.[66] This kind of belief requires action. One may not merely assent mentally and not at least endeavor to "walk as he walked"[67] and then claim to be a believer.

The true path is a narrow one. "Because strait[68] is the gate, and narrow is the way, which leadeth unto life, and few there be that find it."[69] But if we keep seeking diligently, we will find it.[70] As Rebbe Nachman of Breslov famously said, "All the world is a very narrow bridge, and the most important thing is not to be overwhelmed by fear." As we walk the narrow path, we have confidence "that, if we ask any thing according to his will, he heareth us:"[71] As we truly seek Yehovah, we will be guided to the narrow path. I suggest that those who would broaden the path so as not to live by Torah are trying to enter via the wide gate on the broad path "that leadeth to destruction, and many there be which go in thereat:"[72]

Therefore, it is not by any claim to divinity that Yeshua claims to be the way, truth and life, but as the God's agent, so living the Word as to be the Word made flesh.

I AM – *EGO EIMI*

Greek verbs, unlike English, do not usually require a pronoun to indicate person or number. Many modern languages work the same way. In the Taco Bell commercial, for example, the chihuahua did

66. Bullinger, *Companion*, appendix 104.
67. 1 John 2:6.
68. "Strait" is a synonym for narrow, as in the Straits of Gibraltar, a narrowing of the Mediterranean Sea forming the border between the Med and the Atlantic.
69. Matt 7:14.
70. Luke 11:9.
71. 1 John 5:14.
72. Matt 7:13.

not need the pronoun "yo" in his statement, "*Yo quiero* Taco Bell." The "O" suffix in "*quiero*" implies "*yo*" and not "*tu*" or "*usted.*" To say, "I am fine" in Greek one would say "*eimi kala.*" Literally, that is "am fine," with the pronoun implied. That would be proper Greek, but not good English.

Adding the pronoun to say, "*ego eimi,*" makes the statement more emphatic, "I am he." Trinitarians claim that to say "*ego eimi*" is to claim to be divine. They relate Yeshua's statement to the Pharisees, " . . . Before Abraham was I am,"[73] to God speaking to Moses saying, "I am that I am . . . tell them I am sent me to you."[74] The argument goes something like this: God calls Himself "I am," Jesus said, "I am," therefore Jesus is God.

The conversation between God and Moses at the burning bush included this excerpt:

> And Moses said unto God, Behold, when I come unto the children of Israel, and shall say unto them, The God of your fathers hath sent me unto you; and they shall say to me, What is his name? what shall I say unto them?
> And God said unto Moses, I AM THAT I AM: and he said, Thus shalt thou say unto the children of Israel, I AM hath sent me unto you.
> And God said moreover unto Moses, Thus shalt thou say unto the children of Israel, The LORD God of your fathers, the God of Abraham, the God of Isaac, and the God of Jacob, hath sent me unto you: this is my name for ever, and this is my memorial unto all generations.[75]

"I am that I am" in Hebrew is "*ehyeh asher ehyeh.*" *Ehyeh* is the Qal imperfect form of the verb "*hayah,*" "to be." The *aleph* prefix "*eh*" indicates first person, singular. "Imperfect" relates to the action of the verb. It indicates incomplete or continuing action. God calls himself *Ehyeh*, meaning I always am; My being never ends. The name *Yehovah* (*Yud, Heh, Vav, Heh*) is a contraction of *Hayah, Hoveh, Y'hyeh*, He [always] was, He [now] is, He [always]

---

73. John 8:58.
74. Exod 3:14.
75. Exod 3:13–15.

Re-Examining Misconstrued Passages in Light of Hebrew Reasoning

will be. Some translations of *Tanakh* (Hebrew Scriptures) and *siddurim* (prayer books) translate the name YHVH as "The Eternal [One]." When YHVH is translated as "Lord," the o, r, and d are commonly in small capitals to distinguish the Name from other words that mean "lord," such as *adon* or *kyrios*.

"I am" is simply YHVH in first person, singular. *Yehovah* is the Creator's name forever,[76] not *Ehyeh*.

The Septuagint renders, " . . . say . . . *Ehyeh* hath sent . . . " not as "say *ego eimi* sent me," but "say *ho on* sent me." Not "Say I am sent me," but "say the Being [One] sent me," the Eternal One sent me, He Who was, Who is, and Who will be sent me.

In one of his frequent arguments with religious leaders, Yeshua tells them, "Your father Abraham rejoiced to see my day: and he saw *it* and was glad."[77] They misinterpreted him, once again, as claiming to have been contemporary with Abraham, nearly 2000 years before. He replied, "Verily, verily, I say unto you, Before Abraham was, I am."[78]

Trinitarians claim that the statement "I am," is a claim of divinity. If so, then the Man Born Blind[79] also claimed to be God.

> The neighbours therefore, and they which before had seen him that he was blind, said, Is not this he that sat and begged?
> Some said, This is he: others said, He is like him: but he said, *I am he*.[80]

In this verse, the Greek text translated "I am he" is *ego eimi*, "I am." The assertion that saying "*ego eimi*" is a claim to deity cannot be supported. It is a grasping at straws to manufacture evidence for an unbiblical, I suggest even an *anti*biblical, doctrine.

"Before Abraham was . . . " is also poorly translated. "Was" is *genesthai*, the second aorist, middle deponent infinitive of

---

76. Ex 3:15.
77. John 8:56.
78. John 8:58.
79. John 9:1–11.
80. John 9:8–9, emphasis added.

ginomai, come to be.[81] "Before Abraham comes to be, I am." When will Abraham come to be? In the Resurrection at the end of days.

Yeshua promises that his followers "shall never see death."[82] His opponents challenge that statement with "Abraham is dead, and the prophets.... Art thou greater than our father Abraham?" After the Resurrection those who enter the life of the age to come will never [again] see death. Clearly, it is not that those who "keep his sayings" will never see death in this life.

A better rendering of this verse, in light of its culture and context, might be, "Before Abraham comes to be [again in the resurrection] I am [already resurrected]."[83]

BAPTIZING IN THE NAME

In what is called the Great Commission, Yeshua instructed his disciples, saying,

> All power is given unto me in heaven and in earth. Go ye therefore, and teach all nations, baptizing them in the name of the Father, and of the Son, and of the Holy Ghost: Teaching them to observe all things whatsoever I have commanded you: and, lo, I am with you alway, even unto the end of the world. Amen.[84]

First of all, if he had all power from eternity, when was it given to him? Next, he tells them to teach all nations baptizing them "in the name of the Father, and of the Son, and of the Holy Ghost." Some have questioned the authenticity of this verse, since never in the Book of Acts do the disciples use this formula; they always baptize "in the name of the Lord," or "in the name of the Lord Jesus."

While scholars tend to agree that this verse is original, there is nothing in the formula to suggest a triune being of any sort. As

---

81. Blue Letter, *John* 8:58.
82. John 8:51–53.
83. Buzzard, *Posts*.
84. Matt 28:18–20.

we discussed above, the Hebrew concept of agency explains the passage better than the imported Platonic trinity. Brown points out that the mere mention of three persons in the same sentence in no way suggests that they are triune, any more than Dorothy and her friends' fear of "lions and tigers and bears, oh, my," suggests a triune beast[85] which is fully lion, fully tiger and fully bear.

---

85. Brown, *Misgod'ed*, 127.

Reformations

WHEN THE PROTESTANT REFORMATION began early in the 16th century, the Reformers dragged so much Nicene baggage along that they could never achieve escape velocity. Just as the Greek philosophers in the early Nazarean Movement before them, they simply left unexamined many doctrines which they imported. As a result, Protestantism continued sitting in rows of pews, watching the trained professionals. They continued to distinguish between a clergy class and the laity. They kept the Greco-Roman speculation on the nature of God, still rejecting the Hebraic concept that one means one. They continued in Replacement Theology, which leads to antisemitism. (How can people worship as God the most famous Jew ever to walk the face of the earth, and then hate Jews?) They continued gathering to worship on the Venerable Day of the Unconquered Sun.

This is not to disparage the great work the Reformers accomplished. It is only to say that there is still much to be done. They barely scratched the surface.

Among the unexamined doctrinal baggage they dragged along was a belief in the authority of the Church to burn heretics. The Protestant churches had not reformed their doctrine by much when the Calvinists burned Michael Servetus at the stake for heresy.[1]

---

1. The Calvinists' alliance with the Jesuits against the Unitarians proved to be short sighted. Once it is granted that the State may legitimately enforce religious doctrine, the only thing that matters is Who controls the State? The

Reformations

In short, it was impossible to "reform" the church to "primitive Christianity" since what is commonly called the "Church" is quite unrelated to the original Nazarean Movement.

During the Second Great Awakening of the early 19th century, some movements tried to eliminate articles of faith. Among these were the Unitarian movement and the Stone-Campbell "Restoration" movement. Individuals were expected and empowered to read the Bible and reach their own conclusions. There were slogans in circulation like "no creed but Christ; no book but the Bible;" and "in essentials unity, in non-essentials liberty, and in all things harmony." The Bible was so much a part of American culture that no one was considered educated without a thorough familiarity with the sacred text.

With this great liberty comes great responsibility. Proficiency in the Bible takes work, hard work. Many do not have the leisure to study sufficiently. (The English word "scholar" comes from a Greek root meaning "leisure.") There is a tendency to rely on experts, in which case a creed or set of articles is attractive. Or, since anyone's opinion is just as acceptable as anyone else's, no matter how badly informed, the temptation arises to base a position on the merest cursory scan of the text.

Jesuits had been sent into Poland and the surrounding states to win them back to the Roman Catholic Church from Protestantism. Rather than fight ideas with persuasion, forces of Rome installed agents in the royal court. The Inquisition then moved against Protestant sects in order from weakest to strongest. The Calvinists, believing that theirs was the only true Church, and that believing Trinitarian doctrine was necessary for salvation, cheerfully persecuted Unitarians. They believed, as did the Inquisition, that non-Trinitarians were worse than murderers. Murderers could only take a temporal life, while "heretics" deprived their "victims" of eternal life. The Jesuits and the Calvinists shared a belief that by killing Unitarians, they were "doing God service." After the Unitarians and the Bretheren and the Lutherans, the Inquisition turned on their erstwhile allies, the Calvinists. The Calvinists, having established the precedent that burning heretics is a legitimate function of government, were estopped from asserting that they are more entitled to religious liberty than the sects they themselves had persecuted. Thus, Poland was purged of Protestantism. The enemy of my enemy in not necessarily my friend.

For example, many casual readers see in the Lake of Fire in the Book of the Revelation[2] a similarity with the version of Hell they were taught as children in Sunday school. They conclude that the doctrine of Hell that they were taught is supported by Scripture and that the Lake of Fire *is* Hell. If the reader paid a little more attention, he would see that Rev 20:14 (KJV) says, "And death and hell were cast into the lake of fire. This is the second death." Hell is not going to be thrown into Hell. Hell will be destroyed.[3]

All too often, one's religious education stalls at the age of *bar mitzvah*, confirmation, or believer baptism. Few become "Bereans."

The Unitarian movement in America began as Biblical literalists. By reading and studying Scripture, they concluded that the Bible teaches that God is a singular Unity, not a compound Trinity. By allowing the use of reason, they nearly became the dominant opinion in American Christianity. Unfortunately, the Transcendentalism of thinkers like Ralph Waldo Emerson infiltrated the movement. The Gospel of the Kingdom was replaced by the Social Gospel.

Similarly, the Stone-Campbell movement which became the Christian Church (Disciples of Christ) allowed for liberty of doctrine. Eventually, the movement split into three: the Church of Christ (best known for prohibiting instrumental music at services), the Christian Church (Disciples of Christ), and the Independent Christian Churches. As each of the three is congregationally governed, there will be exceptions to any generalization.

The Church of Christ and the Independents tend to be conservative and have generally adopted creedal statements consonant with mainstream Nicene tradition, thus leaving the Unitarianism of Alexander Campbell. The Disciples still do not impose a creed. They have moved toward the "progressive" end of the spectrum, and do not recognize as much authority in the Scriptures as did

---

2. Rev 19:20, 20:10, 14–15.

3. There is much more to consider on this point, which is beyond the scope of this small book. The King James translators were not always careful to distinguish between *hades* and *gehenna* when choosing to render them as "hell," for example.

their founders. In many congregations they have reincorporated trinitarian liturgical elements, such as the Doxology and *Gloria Patri*, though they do not require that members believe in the Trinity.

There is a new reformation going on now.[4] Light which was lost is being regained in reverse order to its loss. The priesthood of the believer which was lost to the professional clergy class is being rediscovered. The singular unity of the Creator is making a comeback. The full humanity of the Second Adam is revived. The Hebrew hope of resurrection[5] is being restored to its rightful place, supplanting Greek speculation of an immortal soul. Those who undertake to live according to Torah find it a delight, as did King David.[6] Torah as a schoolmaster is leading people to the Messiah;[7] the Messiah is leading people to the Father. The Creator's great name is being proclaimed to the world.[8] [9] Followers of Yeshua are returning to the Feasts of Yehovah, leaving behind the holidays borrowed from Sun-god worship. Yehovah is energizing and strengthening His remnant as the End of Days approaches.

This return to basics is flying mostly under the radar of the religious mainstreams. Torben Sondergard[10] predicts that the current underground revival will be the last before the end of the age. Historian David Barton says that when there is widespread revival, rarely will the mainstream church be a part of it until very late in the process. He points out that standard-brand ministers advised their parishioners to avoid both the First and Second Great Awakenings.[11]

In similar fashion, the Jesus Movement of the late 1960s and 70s generally found its fertile ground in living rooms and coffee

---

4. Sondergarrd, *Last*.
5. My Jewish Learning, *Resurrection*.
6. Ps 1:2, 119:70; 77, 92, 172.
7. Gal 3:24.
8. Johnson, *Hallowed*.
9. Gordon, *Shattering*.
10. Sondergarrd, *Last*, 16.
11. Barton, *Schoolhouse*.

houses. The various ministries billed themselves as "parachurch" ministries to assuage the inevitable resistance from mainstream pastors. They didn't seek to replace the regular church, they said, but to supplement it.

In these days when almost anyone can publish on the internet, practically for free, ideas which would have been suppressed by editors of established publishing houses can be made available to pretty much the entire world, unorthodox and pre-orthodox notions can find their niches in the marketplace. The counter-reformationist forces of orthodoxy cannot simply burn books and heretics in the town square as did their spiritual ancestors during the Great Reformation of the European Renaissance.

As Luther, *et al.* demonstrated, a reformer always starts out as a heretic. He can stay and attempt to reform his organization, or he can leave and start something new. As a practical matter, someone who fails to toe the party line will likely be expelled if he does not leave of his own accord.

Myriad groups and ministries have sprung up in recent years. Many individuals are leaving their congregations and forming new fellowships in their homes. There is an awakening to the model of the first generation of followers of the *Maggid* of Nazareth. Some are rediscovering Torah, how it is a delight and not an unbearable burden, as many suppose. Some are rediscovering the manifestation of the spirit, how healing and prophecy, etc., are still in force, and have not yet ceased. Some are rediscovering the sweetness of an egalitarian home fellowship in contrast to the rigidity of hierarchical denominational polity. And perhaps most importantly, some are rediscovering the humanity of the Man Approved of God.

Some are discovering the disutility of creeds, confessions, and articles of faith. Home fellowships are freeing themselves from denominational hierarchies. Reactionary forces of orthodoxy consider these developments as dangerous. Home fellowshippers are finding that these developments provide the opportunity to "test everything," like Bereans. Uniformity of doctrine is among the earliest blunders of the proto-orthodox church and may well be the last major error corrected.

Reformations

What follows is a sampling of teachers, ministries, organizations who, in my opinion, are a part of this (possibly last) reformation. A mention is not necessarily and endorsement. It is safe to say that I probably agree with some but not all of the positions of anyone mentioned. There are others, no doubt that I do not mention. This does not indicate any lack of endorsement; it may mean that I have simply not heard of them.

TORAH OBSERVANT

Biblical Foundations Academy, International

BFA International produces materials for people who seek a biblical foundation for their faith. The three pillars of the Academy are the Creator's Time, Torah and Tetragrammaton. Without a foundation in God's word as revealed in the Hebrew Scriptures, one cannot properly understand the New Testament writings. The Creator's calendar, His instruction (Torah) on how to live righteously in this world and His (four-letter) Name the Tetragrammaton (YHVH) are necessary elements of a biblical foundation.

119 Ministries

Audio and video teachings from 119 Ministries begin with this introduction:

> Hello, and welcome to another teaching from 119 Ministries. Our ministry believes that the whole Bible is true and directly related to our lives today . . . We hope you enjoy studying and testing the following teaching.

119's on-camera speakers do not generally identify themselves; they believe that the message is what is important, not the messenger. Since Yeshua taught that the Torah would stand forever, even if Heaven and earth pass away, they endeavor to live according to the Creator's instructions. The word Torah means

Instruction. It is their response of obedience, and not as so many Christians think, trying to earn salvation.

New2Torah

Zachary Bauer was raised in a traditional Protestant church. He discovered that the Dispensationalism he was taught results in contradictions which are resolved if the Torah is still operative. His site is dedicated to providing simple instruction to people who are, as the name says, new to Torah-observance. Doing what the Torah says is much easier than most Christians think, and much simpler than Rabbinic *halacha* would suggest. He searches for other Torah teachers to recommend to his listeners, and he himself teaches the simplicity that is Torah. He ends each of his videos with, "Go home. Read your Bible."

A Rood Awakening

Michael Rood, founder of A Rood Awakening, takes a no-nonsense approach to Scripture. He has occasionally been described as abrasive. This, he says, is deliberate, as he is not interested in merely entertaining people who like to have their ears tickled. His magnum opus is his *The Chronological Gospels*, which arranges the events of Yeshua's 70-week (not three-and-a-half-year) ministry in chronological order to the exact date, and sometimes to the hour.

ARA also publishes the "Astronomically and Agriculturally Corrected Biblical Hebrew Calendar." The biblical calendar was based on actual observation of the new moon, and the ripening of the barley harvest. The current Jewish calendar is based on calculations made by Hillel II, the last *Nasi* of the Sanhedrin in 359CE. Their corrected calendar returns to Torah based observations.

CHARISMATIC

The Last Reformation

Jesus said that the people who believed in him would do all works he did and more (some versions say "greater").[12] Torben Sondergarrd takes this literally. Unlike many other Charismatic ministries, he takes newly baptized believers out on the street immediately to evangelize and pray for people.

Wildfire Ministries Global

Those who worship God must worship in spirit and in truth.[13] Robert Wilkinson of Wildfire has written short books about believers manifesting that holy spirit which is God's gift of new birth. Holy spirit is the gift; manifesting the gift is the privilege of every disciple. Where there is much spirit and little truth, there is a great danger of counterfeit. Wilkinson teaches people how to manifest properly according to the Word of God.

BIBLICAL UNITARIAN

Spirit and Truth Fellowship

Spirit and Truth Fellowship is a para-church ministry. Its mission is to provide teaching and resources to local assemblies and individuals. They provide books, blogs, and speakers. Their video teachings are available through their subsidiary website, truthortradition.com. Spirit and Truth publishes the Revised English Version of the Bible, with copious footnotes online. The work continues with new notes added periodically. A hard copy is available for purchase.

---

12. John 14:12.
13. John 4:24.

Restoration Fellowship

Founded by Sir Anthony Buzzard, a leading Biblical Unitarian of the day, Restoration Fellowship seeks to restore "Primitive Christianity," as it was practiced·in the first century CE. The name recalls the Restoration Movement, which was a significant part of the Second Great Awakening of the early 19th century. Barton Stone and Alexander Campbell, who each had large followings joined their groups together with a handshake, rather than through creedal statements, which they saw as dividing and not unifying. Sir Anthony also suggests that we abandon creeds devised by church councils and return to Jesus' own creed: Hear, O Israel, the LORD is our God the LORD is one.

Teileios Ministries

Billing itself as "for the mature members of the Body of Christ," Teileios is a repository of in-depth research and teaching. They reproduce some of the classical theological works of such Unitarians as Isaac Newton and Joseph Priestley (both of whom are better known for their scientific discoveries); Ground-breaking books by Bullinger, Wierwille, Boyle and Locke are available. Aside from their Unitarian position, they also have classic writings on the manifestation of the spirit (commonly and erroneously called "gifts"). Teileios' strong meat is not recommended for the neophyte still accustomed to the milk of the Word.

OTHER

Naturist Christians

Rejecting the Gnostic dualism which infects much of the mainstream church, Christian naturists believe that what God made, formed, and created is "very good," and it dishonors the Creator to treat His creation as shameful. Humans were designed to live "naked and unashamed" in the Garden. The Garden is not currently accessible, but human physiology has not changed. Those whose sins are remitted have no need for body shame. Living a lifestyle as close to Edenic as practicable is part of their program of living in harmony with the Creator.

Far from inciting lust, chaste nudity actually inhibits lustful thoughts. Lust begins in the imagination. When the imagination is overruled by the eyes, the opportunity for lust is diminished. It may seem counterintuitive, but clothing is counterproductive as a means to curb impure thoughts. The essence of modesty is in not attracting attention to oneself. It is not in the amount of skin one hides.

Conclusion

LEADERS OF NICENE CHRISTIANITY require adherents to believe certain doctrines, which by their own admissions, are not taught explicitly in Scripture and cannot be understood by mortal humans. Since the Scriptures do not voluntarily support many of these doctrines, the sacred text must be massaged to make it appear to do so. Passages have been added, altered, mispunctuated, and mistranslated in order to force human dogmas. Greek notions such as trinity, immortal soul, pre-existence, immediate afterlife have no place in the Hebrew literature and culture of the New Testament writings. Indeed, there is no relationship whatsoever between post-biblical, Nicene Christianity and first century Nazarean Judaism as taught by Yeshua the *Maggid* of Nazareth and his immediate disciples. The Jesus of orthodoxy is not the same person as the actual, historical, flesh-and-blood Yeshua.

When we return to the Hebraic nature of the New Testament writings, when we learn to think like a Hebrew, when we purge the influence of Greek philosophy from our exegesis, the entire "superstructure" of what is commonly called "Christianity" crumbles like a stale matzah. The dogmas that the church has burned people alive for merely questioning simply vanish.

The good news is, that while the mainstream of Protestantism sleeps in its pews, there is a new underground reformation movement of people who have received a love of the truth and are willing to test everything, even long cherished and formerly unassailable teachings, and hold fast to what is good. Without

Conclusion

mandatory creeds, they are free to adjust their opinions as additional information comes to their attention, as did Apollos when instructed by Priscilla and Aquila.[1]

These independent assemblies are reminiscent of the 17th century Collegiant movement.[2] Collegiants met to discuss religious matters in members' homes. There was complete liberty of conscience; no topic was off-limits. All seekers of Truth were welcome and enjoyed mutual respect. The full spectrum of Protestant thought was represented, from Calvinist Reformed to Anabaptist to Mennonite to Socinian. Even Baruch Spinoza found a home there after he was excommunicated from the Jewish Community. Those orthodox doctrines which can only be defended with violence and not by legitimate exegesis fell by the wayside.

With great liberty comes great responsibility. Believers at liberty to read and understand the Bible for themselves must search the Scriptures like Bereans and follow the evidence wherever it may lead. The danger of liberty without responsibility is manifest in those denominations where Social Gospel has replaced Gospel, where Marx has replaced Moses.

Along with this new reformation of simply reading the Bible and doing what it says, there is always the danger of the counterfeit. Movements like the so-called "New Apostolic Reformation," and the "Word of Faith" movement, sometimes called "name it and claim it" or "prosperity gospel," tend to replace attention to scriptural detail with experiences and "special revelation." We cannot rely on religious fashion to give us Truth. Martin Luther demonstrated that neither can we simply rely on the definitions of orthodoxy for what constitutes "sound doctrine." We must all search the scriptures like the Bereans to see whether what we have been taught is so. We may not abdicate our responsibilities to our "bishops," no matter how expert they may be. We must read Scripture like Karaites, and not simply adopt the *takkanot* and *ma'asim* of the Pharisees, the theologians or the councils. We cannot afford to rely on folk sayings, like Tevye.

1. Acts 18:26.
2. Wilbur, *History*, 588.

There is not a recognized name for this current renewal of the Nazarean Movement. I think that it is a good thing. Once a name is attached, others who cling to traditional error will claim that name for their own denominations as being the "true" whatever-it-is-called. The path is narrow, and there will be few who find it.[3] Even so, "[Yehovah] is near to all them that call upon Him, to all that call upon Him in Truth."[4]

God told Solomon, "If I shut up heaven that there be no rain, or if I command the locusts to devour the land, or if I send pestilence among my people; If my people, which are called by my name, shall humble themselves, and pray, and seek my face, and turn from their wicked ways; then will I hear from heaven, and will forgive their sin, and will heal their land."[5] There is no lack of pestilence today in our land. How God's people respond is an uncontrolled variable. In our polarized and divided world today, we could be headed into the "time of Jacob's Trouble," or we could be on the cusp of the next Great Awakening. Time will tell.

---

3. Matt 7:14.
4. Ps 145:18.
5. 2 Chr 7:14–15.

Appendix 1
Baptism Formulae

THE TRINITARIAN-SOUNDING BAPTISM FORMULA in Matthew 28:19, "Go ye therefore, and teach all nations, baptizing them in the name of the Father, and of the Son, and of the Holy Ghost:" has been questioned by textual critics. While this version is well attested in the Greek manuscripts, any time a baptism is mentioned in Acts the formula is never used. Rather, they baptize "in the name of the Lord."

Here is a list of verses where the Apostles mention baptism:

- Acts 2:38 "Then Peter said unto them, Repent, and be baptized every one of you in the name of Jesus Christ for the remission of sins, and you shall receive the gift of the Holy Ghost."

- Acts 8:12 "But when they believed Philip preaching the things concerning the kingdom of God, and the name of Jesus Christ, they were baptized, both men and women."

- Acts 8:16 "For as yet he was fallen upon none of them: only they were baptized in the name of the Lord Jesus."

- Acts 10:48 "And he commanded them to be baptized in the name of the Lord. Then prayed they him to tarry certain days."

- Acts 19:5 "When they heard this, they were baptized in the name of the Lord Jesus."

Appendix 1

- Acts 22:16 "And now why tarriest thou? arise, and be baptized, and wash away your sins, calling on the name of the Lord."
- Romans 6:3 "Know you not, that so many of us as were baptized into Jesus Christ were baptized into his death?"
- 1 Corinthians 1:13 "Is Christ divided? was Paul crucified for you? or were you baptized in the name of Paul?"
- Galatians 3:27 "For as many of you as have been baptized into Christ have put on Christ."

Appendix 2
Why most Jews do not consider claims for Jesus as Messiah.

FIRST OF ALL, MOST Jews will never consider a claim of Messiahship for one in whose name they have suffered oppression for many centuries. After pogroms, forced conversions, and less than second class status in Christendom one asks, how could a Jewish Messiah hate Jews so much? Simply, he would not.

Martin Luther suggested being nice to Jews. Maybe then they would be more likely to convert. Jewish cultural memory was longer than his experiment. When Jews continued to decline to convert, Luther reverted to even more vicious antisemitism than before. German Lutherans carried anti-Semitic baggage with them when they broke with the Roman Catholic Church.

This legacy eventually culminated in the Holocaust. Hitler was no Christian, but from a Jewish perspective, all European Gentiles were at least nominally Christian. The terms Christian and Gentile were essentially interchangeable in the European Jewish community.

Next, as we have seen above, Nicene Christianity misrepresents the *Maggid* of Nazareth. Christians side with his enemies when they accuse him of claiming to be God. There is variety in Jewish expectation about the Messiah. There is unanimity in the expectation that he will be a human and not divine. Most Jews

Appendix 2

rightly consider worshipping a man as though he were God to be idolatry.

Finally, but not exhaustively, Christians overstate their claim. It is claimed that Jesus fulfilled over 300 explicit messianic prophecies.[1] Having fulfilled these prophecies, he must be the Messiah. The problem is that most of these "prophecies" are neither explicit nor as obvious as claimed. They were not even obvious to disciples who knew Yeshua personally. Let us look at the conversation on the Road to Emmaus:

> And, behold, two of them went that same day to a village called Emmaus, which was from Jerusalem about threescore furlongs. And they talked together of all these things which had happened. And it came to pass, that, while they communed together and reasoned, Jesus himself drew near, and went with them. But their eyes were holden that they should not know him.
>
> And he said unto them, What manner of communications are these that ye have one to another, as ye walk, and are sad?
>
> And the one of them, whose name was Cleopas, answering said unto him, Art thou only a stranger in Jerusalem, and hast not known the things which are come to pass there in these days?
>
> And he said unto them, What things? And they said unto him, Concerning Jesus of Nazareth, which was a prophet mighty in deed and word before God and all the people:
>
> And how the chief priests and our rulers delivered him to be condemned to death, and have crucified him.
>
> But we trusted that it had been he which should have redeemed Israel: and beside all this, to day is the third day since these things were done.
>
> Yea, and certain women also of our company made us astonished, which were early at the sepulchre;
>
> And when they found not his body, they came, saying, that they had also seen a vision of angels, which said that he was alive.

---

1. newtestamentchristians.com, *Prophecies*.

Appendix 2

> And certain of them which were with us went to the sepulchre, and found it even so as the women had said: but him they saw not.
>
> Then he said unto them, O fools, and slow of heart to believe all that the prophets have spoken: Ought not Christ to have suffered these things, and to enter into his glory?
>
> And beginning at Moses and all the prophets, he expounded unto them in all the scriptures the things concerning himself. [2]

These two disciples had watched Yeshua's ministry firsthand, yet they still failed to connect the dots which many Christians claim are "obvious," until the prophets' words were explained to them.

Some of the claims include: the prediction that the "seed of the woman" will bruise the head of the serpent predicts Messiah's virgin birth; God taking Enoch predicts Messiah's ascension into Heaven; He would be thirsty; God substituting a ram for Isaac predicts the Lamb of God. None of these passages explicitly refer to the coming Messiah. At most, they are hints and foreshadows which only become clear when they are revealed. When Simon Peter said, "Thou art the Christ, the Son of the living God," It was because that had been revealed to him.[3] It was not particularly obvious.

It is claimed that referring to Eve's offspring as her seed indicates that Messiah would be born of a virgin, because women do not have seed. This does not bear scrutiny. When Rebekah left her family of origin to marry Isaac, "they blessed Rebekah, and said unto her, Thou art our sister, be thou the mother of thousands of millions, and let thy seed possess the gate of those which hate them."[4] Seed simply refers to offspring, descendants. It is the same word for descendants of a man as for descendants of a woman.

---

2. Luke 24:13–27.
3. Matt 16:16–17.
4. Gen 24:60.

APPENDIX 2

When God "took" Enoch, it is assumed that He took him to Heaven without dying. This assumption presupposes that those who have died are alive in either Heaven or Hell immediately after the end of this life. We have seen above that such is not the case. Rather the dead are "asleep" pending resurrection and judgment. Neither in Genesis nor in Hebrews does the Bible say where God took Enoch, only that He transferred him from where he was. After listing great heroes of faith, the writer of Hebrews continues with "These all died in faith . . . ."[5] All includes both Enoch and Elijah,[6] both of whom are commonly thought to have never died.

The protagonist in Psalm 22 speaks of his "strength" being dried up.[7] This is taken as a prediction which was fulfilled when Jesus said, "I thirst."[8] The connection is far from clear. Indeed, who has not experienced occasional thirst?

When God instructed Abraham to offer Isaac, He arranged to substitute a ram in Isaac's place.[9] John the Baptist identifies Jesus as "the Lamb of God."[10] A ram and a lamb are both sheep, but the ram is an adult and the lamb is a juvenile. The analogy breaks down if it is stretched too thin.

Some passages which are taken for messianic prophecies do not say what many think they say. When missionaries use these verses to convince someone who is familiar with the Hebrew original, they wind up looking foolish.

Psalm 22:16 (KJV) says "For dogs have compassed me: the assembly of the wicked have inclosed me: they pierced my hands and my feet." Crucifixion entails nailing the prisoner's hands and feet to the cross, necessarily piercing them. In the original Hebrew,

---

5. Heb 11:12.

6. When we read about the chariot took Elijah into "heaven," (2 Kgs 2:11) we need to remember that *shamayim* can be rendered as "heaven" or "sky." The context and scope of the Scriptures determines the translation. The Scripture does not record where the chariot landed.

7. Ps 22:15.

8. John 19:28.

9. Gen 22:13.

10. John 1:29, 36.

Appendix 2

however, the Psalmist compares his enemies to a pack of dogs surrounding him, to a wicked gang circling him, *like a lion* at his hands and feet (emphasis added).

The word rendered "they pierced" is *ka'ari*. The K' prefix means "like" *ari* means "lion." *Ari* (aleph-resh-yod) is the root. The King James version renders *ka'ari* as though the root were *karah*, (caph-resh-heh) to dig, excavate, bore.

Fortunately, many later translations read "like a lion" rather than "they pierced."

Isaiah 7:14 (KJV) presents a sign, "A virgin shall conceive and bear a son . . . ." This does not match the Hebrew which reads "The young woman is pregnant and is bearing a son." Jewish tradition says that the young woman was Isaiah's wife. This child is already in gestation when the oracle is given. Before the child grows to learn right from wrong (v. 16), the kings of the enemy lands currently threatening Judah will be gone.

There are two words in Hebrew commonly translated as "virgin." There is *almah* which is a young woman of marriageable age or recently married. And there is *bethulah* which is an intact virgin. Both are rendered *parthenos* in the Septuagint. Mary is called *parthenos* in the birth narrative in Luke 1:27.

Marriage license applications in American jurisdictions typically ask the parties' current status, whether single, widowed, or divorced. In some other English-speaking jurisdictions, they ask bride's status whether "virgin," widowed, or divorced. They are not asking about her purity, but whether she has been previously married.

This prophecy does not predict that the Messiah would be born of an intact virgin, nor does it rule the idea out. Whatever hints there may be about the Messiah, they are hints, and not explicit predictions. Yeshua said that the Scriptures speak of him,[11] but even his closest disciples did not always understand what they foretold of him.

When Christians make claims of Scripture which the Scripture does not support, they undermine their witness. When a

---

11. John 5:39.

Appendix 2

potential Jewish convert, especially one well versed in the Hebrew Scriptures, exposes these commonly repeated errors, he will be less likely than before to hear the Gospel of the Kingdom from those who, however innocently, misrepresent it.

All of these foreshadowings might indeed be hints, but they are not obvious, explicit predictions of the life of the Messiah. Looking back, with a Messiah candidate in mind, one might tease out a subtle predictive interpretation. But looking forward, they only tell the stories of the ancients. Most Jews do not find these arguments persuasive. Again, Christians appear to oversell their case, which only weakens it.

The writer of Hebrews[12] famously called Yehovah's Feasts a shadow picture of good things to come. This prompts some to ask, "Why keep the shadow now that Messiah has come?" When we compare the silhouette of the Hellenized, so-called second person of the Trinity with the shadow cast by the appointed times, we see that they do not match. On the other hand, the silhouette of Yeshua, the Jewish Messiah does indeed match the shadow pictures.

In the opening of *Alfred Hitchcock Presents* on television, the viewer sees an outline of Mr. Hitchcock in profile and hears Charles Gounod's *Funeral March of a Marionette*. Hitchcock's shadow moves in from out of frame and matches the outline. If we heard, for example, Fucik's *Entry of the Gladiators*, (best known as clown music in the circus) and saw Don Knotts' (best known for playing Deputy Barney Fife) shadow, we would know that we are not watching *Alfred Hitchcock Presents*, but a comic parody. Similarly, when we see Passover replaced by Easter, the Fall Feasts replaced by Christmas, Sabbath replaced by the Venerable Day of the Unconquered Sun, we know that we no longer have the faith and practice of Yeshua and his disciples, but a tragic parody.

The Exodus from Egypt is the foundational narrative for Judaism. Sabbath is a reminder of the work of Creation and of our departure from Egypt. The Passover season is called the Season of our Joy, where families gather at the Seder to tell and retell every year the story of our deliverance. The story of a Jewish Messiah

12. Heb 10:1.

Appendix 2

would necessarily be predicated on the story of the Exodus, so that Jewish people would recognize his story as Jewish.

When the Hebrews were in Egypt, conditions went from pretty good to not so good to bad to worse. When things got really bad, in the fullness of time, the People cried out to God, and God heard their prayer. As He had planned from the beginning, God brought judgment on Egypt, and the People were suddenly brought out. When things get really bad in end of this age, and judgment is about to be poured out on the Earth, God's People will again be delivered suddenly and in the fullness of time in what is commonly referred to as the Rapture.

Joel Richardson in his recent *Sinai to Zion*,[13] assembles the puzzle pieces from the Prophets and traces the path of Messiah's conquering army in the end times as it follows the path of the Israelites leaving Egypt to the conquest of the Promised Land. To anyone conversant with the original Exodus, the eventual career of the Messiah Triumphant will be unmistakable.

Not all of the "good things to come" which the Feasts foreshadow have yet happened. We still need the shadows to give us the general outline of those good things, so we will not be deceived by a counterfeit. Muslims and Christians both have a vision of a coming Ruler; each side thinks that its Ruler is the genuine and the other's is the Deceiver. By comparing these men with the "shadow pictures," we will be able to know which is which.

Most Christians condense the career of Jesus into the words of the creeds, "He was conceived of the Holy Ghost, born of the Virgin Mary, suffered under Pontius Pilate, was crucified, dead and buried, and on the third day rose again." There is nothing in the Creeds about his ministry on Earth, nothing to connect him to the Jewish People. As Gordon points out,[14] The Christian Jesus looks more like a Greek demigod than a Jewish Messiah. It is no wonder that most Jews will not consider Christian claims for Jesus.

---

13. Richardson, *Sinai*.
14. Gordon, *Hebrew*.

Appendix 3
Some words that have changed meaning

Asia—When "all Asia heard the Word" in two years and three months because of Paul's missionary activity, "Asia" referred to the Roman Province of Asia, about one-third of modern Turkey, not the entire Continent of Asia. While delivering the word to the entire Province of Asia is still an impressive feat, it is not as spectacular as preaching to the entire Continent of Asia.

Lord—American Christians are not in the habit of addressing any mortal human as "my lord." 240-some years ago, we fought a revolution, in part, so we would no longer be obliged to apply that title to men. The words translated "lord" in the Bible, *adon* in Hebrew and *kyrios* in Greek, can be rendered in English as lord, sir, or mister. Informally, "boss" is also appropriate, as in the famous bumper sticker, "My boss is a Jewish carpenter." A modern example of a single word carrying all three meanings is the Spanish word "señor," as in the expressions "Jesu Cristo es el Señor," "Si, Señor," or "Señor Gonzalez." Neither Señor nor Lord are specifically divine titles.

The unfortunate tradition of rendering the Name of God, *Yud-Heh-Vav-Heh* as Lord, even though YHVH is unrelated to *adon* has proven misleading. With no current usage of Lord in American vernacular (except landlord), One can easily fall into the error of assuming that since both God and Jesus are called "lord," then Jesus is God.

Appendix 3

Humans in the Bible are also addressed as *adon*: Abraham, Gen. 8:12, 23:15; Abraham's servant whom he sent to find Isaac a wife, Gen24:18; Laban, Gen 31:35; Esau, Gen 32:4; Joseph as Prime Minister of Egypt, Gen 44:5, 7, 16, 18, &c.; Moses, by his brother Aaron, Gen 32:22, and many others. Humans are also called *kyrios*: a "certain man" in a parable, Luke 14:23; a vineyard owner in another parable, Luke 20:13; any boss, John 15:15, 20. This list is not exhaustive.

Lord's Day/Day of the Lord—As used in *Tanakh*, the Hebrew Scriptures, the Day of the Lord is the time of Yehovah's judgment. The proud will be brought down.[1] Sinners will be destroyed out of the Holy Land.[2] It will be His day of vengeance.[3] The heavens will pass away and the elements melt.[4] The Day of the Lord, the Lord's day, is not Sunday, it is Judgment Day.

The only place where the exact phrase, "the Lord's day" appears in KJV is Rev 1:10. John writes, "I was in the Spirit on the Lord's day," and continues to describe the coming Judgment. Later church tradition adopted the day dedicated to Dominus Sol Invictus, the day of the Lord Unconquered Sun-god and applied the term "the Lord's Day" to Sunday conveniently omitting to tell us which "lord" Sun-day was dedicated to. Throughout the Hebrew Scriptures, the Day of the Lord is the Day of Wrath and Judgment. We may not ignore biblical definitions of words or phrases when we find the same phrase later in the text.[5] Too often Christians read the New Testament as though it were unrelated to the Old. On the contrary, the Elder Testament, as Rabbi Zalman Schachter-Shalomi says,[6] is the foundation for the Younger Testament.

In the spirit, John was "on the Day of the Lord," not on some particular Sunday.

1. Isa 2:12.
2. Isa 13:6.
3. Jer 46:10.
4. 2 Pet 3:10.
5. See "Consistency of Meaning," Methodology, supra.
6. Zaslow, *Jesus*, Introduction.

Appendix 3

Mystery—Many Christians describe some of their fundamental doctrines as "mysteries," which mere humans cannot possibly comprehend. I like to ask, "If you cannot comprehend your doctrine, how do you know that you believe it correctly?" Paul uses the word mystery, *musterion* in the Greek, to refer to a sacred secret which was hidden until God chose to reveal it, after which it is no longer a mystery.

> And when [Yeshua] was alone, they that were about him with the twelve asked of him the parable. And he said unto them, Unto you it is given to know the mystery of the kingdom of God: but unto them that are without, all these things are done in parables:[7]

Yeshua told his disciples that they would know about the Kingdom of God, but it would remain a mystery, that is unrevealed, to outsiders. Paul builds on this telling us that the mystery which was kept hidden has now been revealed.

- Now to him that is of power to stablish you according to my gospel, and the preaching of Jesus Christ, according to the revelation of the mystery, which was kept secret since the world began, But now is made manifest, and by the scriptures of the prophets, according to the commandment of the everlasting God, made known to all nations for the obedience of faith:[8]

- But we speak the wisdom of God in a mystery, even the hidden wisdom, which God ordained before the world unto our glory: Which none of the princes of this world knew: for had they known it, they would not have crucified the Lord of glory.[9]

- [H]e hath abounded toward us in all wisdom and prudence; Having made known unto us the mystery of his will,

---

7. Mark 4:10–11.
8. Rom 16:25–26.
9. 1 Cor 2:7.

according to his good pleasure which he hath purposed in himself:[10]

- I am made a minister [of the church], according to the dispensation of God which is given to me for you, to fulfil the word of God; Even the mystery which hath been hid from ages and from generations, but now is made manifest to his saints: To whom God would make known what is the riches of the glory of this mystery among the Gentiles; which is Christ in you, the hope of glory:[11]

This list is not exhaustive but serves to demonstrate that once a mystery has been revealed, we are expected to understand it if we have ears to hear and eyes to see. Nowhere are we instructed to believe the incomprehensible, taking "on faith" human pronouncements which even the authorities do not pretend to understand.

Saint—Google Dictionary defines saint as "a person acknowledged as holy or virtuous and typically regarded as being in heaven after death." This is how the term is commonly used in ordinary conversation. This definition does not stand up under biblical scrutiny for two reasons. 1) As we have seen above, the cure for death is the resurrection at the end of days, not an immediate afterlife, and 2) living persons are called saints in both the Old Testament and the New.

Aaron is called "the saint of the LORD."[12] Paul addresses his letters to "To all that be in Rome, beloved of God, called to be saints,"[13] "Unto the church of God which is at Corinth, to them that are sanctified in Christ Jesus, called to be saints,"[14] " . . . to the saints which are at Ephesus,"[15] "to all the saints in Christ Jesus which are at Philippi,"[16] "[t]o the saints and faithful brethren in

10. Eph 1:8–9.
11. Col 1:25–27.
12. Ps 106:16.
13. Rom 1:7.
14. 1 Cor 1:2.
15. Eph 1:1.
16. Phil 1:1.

Appendix 3

Christ which are at Colosse."[17] These letters are addressed to living people, members of the Body of Christ, residing in those cities. There were saints dwelling in Lydda[18] and Jerusalem.[19]

Saint is translated from *hagion* in the Greek of the Septuagint and New Testament, and from *qadosh* in Hebrew. Both words mean "holy." The essence of "holy" is to be "set apart." It could mean set apart from the world or set apart for God. The *Hagia Sophia* Mosque in Istanbul was originally built as a church. Its name can be rendered the Church of Holy Wisdom or the Church of Saint Sophia with equal accuracy.

The saints are living members of the Body of Messiah, who are set apart from the world to serve God.

Worship—The word translated "worship" in the Greek New Testament is *proskuneo*. Derived from *pros*, toward and *kuon*, kiss, it suggests kissing the hand to show subservience, as kissing the hand of the bishop or the Godfather, or a dog licking its master's hand. Strong defines its biblical usage as "to fawn . . . to crouch . . . to prostrate oneself in homage. He also adds "worship."[20]

Those to whom one would "kiss the hand" in the Bible include priests, kings and other potentates, heavenly beings, and of course including but not limited to God. Thus, we see that "worship," as used in the Bible is not necessarily what we think of when we worship God alone. A British magistrate is addressed as "Your Worship." This does not mean that he is God, any more than addressing a Judge of the Queen's Bench (equivalent of an American District Court or Superior Court judge) as "My Lord" means that the Judge is God.

It is good to remember that there are no specifically "spiritual" words. Words used to describe something spiritual are words with visible meanings, used by analogy to the invisible. Even the word "spirit" comes from the Latin *spiritus* which means breath or wind. The wind is an invisible force, which can be felt, but not

17. Col 1:2.
18. Acts 9:32–41.
19. Acts 9:13, 26:10.
20. Strong, *Greek*, 61.

seen. In context, the invisible force of the Spirit of God comes to be named after the Wind, *Ruach*, *Pneuma*, or *Spiritus*.

Appendix 4
Shabbat Dinner

Keeping in mind that there is a wide range of traditions, here is a not uncommon example of Shabbat dinner at home. This is a short form; more traditional communities typically use a much longer one. Usually, it is sung or chanted mostly or all in Hebrew, though any language is acceptable.

A family gathers around the dining room table. They might sing "Shalom Aleichem," "Peace to You:"

> Peace to you ministering angels, messengers of the Most High, coming from the King, the King of Kings, the Holy One, blessed is He.
> Come in peace, messengers of peace, coming from the King, the King of Kings, the Holy One, blessed is He.
> Bless me with peace, messengers of peace, coming from the King, the King of Kings, the Holy One, blessed is He.
> Depart in peace, messengers of peace, coming from the King, the King of Kings, the Holy One, blessed is He.

Then, candles are lit, typically by the Mama of the house and/or the daughters. Anyone may, as long as they are lit. This is a rabbinic ordinance, not found in the written Torah, even though the Blessing calls it a commandment.

> Blessed are You, YHVH our God, King of the universe, Who sanctified us by His commandments and commanded us to kindle the Sabbath light.

Appendix 4

The Kiddush is recited over a cup of wine, typically the Papa, though anyone who is able may lead it.

> There was evening and morning, the sixth day. Thus, the heavens were finished and all their array. On the seventh day God completed the work He had done. God rested on the seventh day from all His work which He had done. God blessed the seventh day and set it apart, because on it He rested from all his work which God created to do.
>
> Blessed are You YHVH our God, King of the universe, Who creates the fruit of the vine.
>
> Blessed are You YHVH our God, King of the Universe, Who sanctifies us with His commandments, Who gave us His holy Sabbath in love and favor as an inheritance to remember Creation. It is the holiest of days, a reminder of our departure from Egypt. You have chosen us and sanctified us from among all the nations, and in love have given us Your holy Sabbath as an inheritance. Blessed are You YHVH, Who sanctifies the Sabbath.

The family drinks the wine.

Ritual handwashing is next. This is another rabbinic ordinance, even though the blessing calls it a commandment. One washes hands by filling a special two-handled pitcher with water, holding the cup in one hand and pouring water over the other hand three times. Then one transfers the pitcher to the other hand, using the other handle, and repeat. The blessing is:

> Blessed are You, YHVH our God, King of the universe, Who sanctified us by His commandments and commanded us concerning the washing of the hands.

Having thus become ritually pure, it is customary to refrain from speaking until the blessing over bread. (It is said that the easiest way to defile oneself is by careless words issuing from the mouth.)

The *challah*, special bread baked for the Sabbath, is uncovered and the blessing recited:

> Blessed are You, YHVH our God, King of the universe, Who brings forth bread from the Earth.

Appendix 4

Then dinner is served and conversation resumes.

After dinner, diners might sing songs, then the *Birkat HaMazon*, the blessing for food is sung or recited:

> When the Lord turned again the captivity of Zion, we were like them that dream. Then was our mouth filled with laughter, and our tongue with singing: then said they among the heathen, The Lord hath done great things for them. The Lord hath done great things for us; whereof we are glad. Turn again our captivity, O Lord, as the streams in the south. They that sow in tears shall reap in joy. He that goeth forth and weepeth, bearing precious seed, shall doubtless come again with rejoicing, bringing his sheaves. with him. (Psalm 126)
>
> [Leader] Friends, let us bless.
>
> [All, then Leader repeats] May the name of YHVH be blessed forever.
>
> [Leader] With the consent of all the friends gathered here, I say: Let us thank our God Whose food we have eaten.
>
> [All, then Leader repeats] Blessed is our God Whose food we have eaten.
>
> [All] Blessed is He and blessed is His name.
>
> Through God's kindness, mercy and compassion all existence is eternally sustained. God is forever faithful. God's surpassing goodness fills all time and space. There is sustenance for all. None ever need lack, no being want for food. We praise you, YHVH, Who sustains all.
>
> As it is written in the Torah: "You shall eat, be satisfied and bless YHVH your God for the good land which He has given you. Blessed are You YHVH for the Earth and for sustenance.
>
> And rebuild Jerusalem, speedily in our day. Blessed are You YHVH, Who in His mercy rebuilds Jerusalem, Amen.
>
> The Merciful One, may He bring us to the time which is all Sabbath rest and the life of the world to come.
>
> He Who makes peace in the heights, may He make peace for us and all Israel, and let us say, Amen.
>
> YHVH gives strength to His people, YHVH blesses His People with peace.

Appendix 4

The custom of Grace *After* Meals comes from the verse quoted above, Deut 8:10, "When thou hast eaten and art full, then thou shalt bless the name of the Lord thy God for the good land which He hath given thee." The Sages, in their wisdom, thought it not a good idea to be long-winded in prayer while the food gets cold. So, they developed a few short blessings before the meal, and more effusive thanks after.

Appendix 5
Humanity

Who is Jesus?

- A *man* approved of God Acts 2:22
- The mediator between God and men, the *man* Christ Jesus. 1 Tim 2:5
- The *man* by whom grace came Rom 5:15
- The last *Adam*. 1 Cor 15:45 (Hebrew adam = human)
- The *Son* of God. Luke 1:35, etc.
- The prophet like Moses, whom God promised to raise up from midst of the Israelites. Deut 18:15; Acts 3:22, 7:37.
- The *Son of Man* Matt 8:20, 9:6, etc.

On the other hand:

- God is not a man . . . nor the son of man. Num 23:19.
- The *Father* is the *only true God*. John 17:3.
- Hear, O Israel: The LORD our God is one LORD: And thou shalt love the lord thy God with all thine heart, and with all thy soul, and with all thy might. Deut 6:4-5; Mark 12:29ff.
- And the LORD shall be king over all the earth: in that day shall there be one LORD, and his name one. Zechariah 14:9.

The Name of Yehovah is One (and not Three.)

Appendix 6
Dispensationalism

DISPENSATIONALISM IS THE THEORY that God's rules change from time to time, according to His divine purpose. Dispensation is how the King James Version translates the Greek word *oikonomia*. It is sometimes rendered administration or economy. The theory was first propounded by John Nelson Darby. C. I. Scholfield popularized the theory in his Chain Reference Bible.

Dispensational theorists usually divide the arc of human history into seven administrations, but the authorities are divided as to when to move from one dispensation to the next. What follows is a list of some of the proposed dispensations.

Paradise: where Adam and Eve dwelt until they sinned.

Conscience: from the expulsion from Eden until the Flood, there were no rules promulgated from Heaven.

Noachide: where the only rules revealed to Mankind were the seven Noachide laws. These laws are not listed in scripture explicitly, they are surmised by Rabbinic sages. This lasted until the Torah was revealed to Moses.

Law: from the Exodus until Jesus' ministry the Torah was binding. Some theorists continue the administration of Law until Pentecost in Acts chapter 2; some hold that Jesus' ministry had its own dispensation.

Christ: Some say that the time when Jesus ministered was its own administration, some say that it was a continuation of the Law administration.

Appendix 6

Apostolic: from the Day of Pentecost until the original Apostles died. Some say that the miracles and prophecy that characterized the ministry of the Apostles have ceased.

Church or *Grace*: from the Day of Pentecost until the future Rapture described in 2 Thessalonians is the age of the Church. It is also called the Age of Grace, wherein one is saved by Grace and not by obedience to the Law, or Torah. Dispensationalists usually believe that Torah has been abolished by Jesus' death and resurrection. Some say that the Law is "held in abeyance" until the end of the Church age and will be reinstated in the Great Tribulation.

Tribulation: Most Evangelicals believe that the Rapture of the Church will be at the end of the Age of Grace. This departure of believers will be the trigger that begins the Tribulation, also called the Great Tribulation. Some theorists hold that the Church will experience the Tribulation and that the Rapture will occur at the end. There is also a theory that the Rapture will occur in the middle of the Tribulation.

Wrath: After the Tribulation and after the Church-Age believers are withdrawn from the Earth, the Wrath of God will be poured out on the wicked as described in the Book of the Revelation.

Millennium: Jesus will reign as King Messiah over the whole Earth from Jerusalem, seated on the throne of his ancestor David.

Paradise restored: where the righteous live eternally with God in Heaven or Paradise.

There are more than seven proposed dispensations listed, and I may not have included every opinion. Different theorists divide the dispensations differently. Some combine two or more into one.

While there is a kernel of truth in dispensationalism, many take the concept to extremes. The theory has been used as a pretext for antinomianism (abolishing Torah) and supercessionism, also called Replacement Theology, where God "rejected the Jews as His Chosen People," since "the Jews rejected Jesus," and replaced Israel with the "Church."

Appendix 7
Unitarian History

I HAVE BEEN ACCUSED by my orthodox Trinitarian friends of making [stuff] up, because they have never heard Unitarian arguments. They are unprepared to "give and answer" for why they believe what they believe. Their teachers have never exposed them to any but the most orthodox opinions.

None of the ideas expressed above are original to me. I have not made any of this up. Indeed, there is a long history of believers who, once they are empowered to read the Scriptures for themselves, come independently to a biblical unitarian position. Some historical examples follow.

Justin Martyr (c. 100–c. 165) Held that the Son is subordinate to the Father. Any deity of the son is derivative of his sonship. This position was proto-orthodox when he wrote it but became retroactively heretical due to the actions of later church councils.

Origen (c. 184–253) reminds us that Messiah is not God but is subordinate to Him.

> [C]are must be taken that no derivative Being be the object of Prayer, no not Christ himself, but only the God and Father of the Universe; to whom also our Saviour himself pray'd . . . as we have elsewhere demonstrated, the Son [is] different as to his Essence from the Father, and subject to him . . . .[1]

---
1. Whiston, *Account*, 73.

Lactantius (240–320) wrote,

> Our Saviour taught that there is but one god, and that he alone is to be worshipped: Nor did he ever say once himself that he was God; .... Wherefore, because he was so faithful, because he assum'd nothing at all to himself, that he might fully perform the Commands of him that sent him; he receiv'd the Dignity of a perpetual priest, and the Honour of the greatest King, and the Power of a Judge, and the Name of God.[2]

Notice that Yeshua received the name of God; it was not his "from Eternity.".

Eusebius (c. 260–c. 340) comments on Christ's derivative deity:

> But if they be afraid lest we seem by any means to preach two Gods, let them know that while the son is confess'd to be God by us; yet there is but One God. He I mean who alone is without beginning, and unbegotten, who in his divinity of himself, and is the Author to the Son himself, both of his Existence and of his existing in so great Dignity; by whom the Son himself owns that he lives, when he plainly says, As the Living Father hath life in himself, so hath he given to the Son to have life in himself.[3]

As the Reformation approached, the dogma of the Trinity came under scrutiny, even among Catholic theologians. Among the orthodox, it was required to be accepted on "blind faith in the Church's authority," even though it was entirely "beyond reason."

Among Protestants, there was more freedom to examine the issue, though Michael Servetus was burned at the stake by Calvinists in 1553 for his Unitarian beliefs.

Rakovian Catechism (1605) The Catechism was produced by the Minor Reformed Church of Poland. They were biblical

---

2. Whiston, *Account*, 71.
3. Whiston, *Account*, 223.

Appendix 7

Unitarians, in that they believed that Yeshua had no divine nature but was given power and authority to act in God's name.[4]

John Locke, in his 1695 classic, *The Reasonableness of Christianity*,[5] reminds us that biblical religion is perfectly reasonable, though many "systems of divinity" are not. Locke also came to a Unitarian understanding of Scripture.

William Whiston published *An Account of the Faith of the First Two Centuries* [6] in 1711. He reproduces writings of first and second century theologians in the original Greek and Latin and provides parallel translations in English. Excerpts from early writers above are from his volume of over 600 pages. He cites Daniel Whitby (1638-1726) and Johannes Ludovicus Wolzogenius (1589-1629) as finding 36 and 60 arguments respectively against the deity of Christ in the Gospel of John, alone. Most Trinitarians claim that John is the New Testament book which most supports their doctrine; these theologians demonstrate that it does not.

He further points out:

> All the Modern Ages have learn'd to call the Father, Son and Holy Ghost *one God*, and say, That these three Divine Persons are *the one God*: Whereas nothing is plainer, as well from the foregoing Testimonies as from all the most ancient Creeds, then that the all the first Christians knew of no other *one God* than the *Father of our Lord Jesus Christ*.

Sir Isaac Newton wrote more about theology than science. As was common of scientists of the time, he regarded science as "God's other book," after the Bible. After his death in 1727, his heirs donated his papers to Cambridge University where he had been a professor. The University accepted his scientific writings but refused his theological works, because he argued against the doctrine of Trinity. His theological works eventually found their way to the National Library of Israel and have only comparatively recently been made available to the public.

4. Britannica, *Racovian*.
5. Locke, *Reasonableness*, 5.
6. Whiston, *Account*.

Appendix 7

Thomas Emlyn (1663–1741) is said to be the first English minister to call himself Unitarian.[7]

Joseph Priestley (1733–1804), in his *An History of the Corruptions of Christianity*,[8] published in 1782, has a section on the development of opinions concerning who Jesus is, beginning with the opinion of his original Jewish followers who called him "a man approved by God," to the eventual Nicene notion of him being both God and man.

V. P. Wierwille (1916–1985) published his book *Jesus Christ is Not God* in 1975.[9]

Sir Anthony Buzzard (b. 1935) commonly remarks that mainstream Christianity has abandoned Jesus' own creed, "Hear O Israel, the Lord is our God, the Lord is One," in favor of incomprehensible man-made creeds. The title of perhaps his most famous book from 1995, *The Doctrine of the Trinity: Christianity's Self-Inflicted Wound*, describes his point sufficiently.

Far from the idea of me "making [stuff] up," the reader can see that there is a long history of Biblical Unitarianism, notwithstanding the claims of the orthodox that "all believers have always held the doctrine of Trinity." On the contrary, Unitarianism is the original and Trinitarianism is the later corruption of the true faith once delivered to the saints.

---

7. Emlyn, *Deity*.
8. Priestley, *History*.
9. Wierwille, *Not God*.

Bibliography

119 Ministries. "The Way—119 Ministries." *YouTube*, June 3, 2014. https://www.youtube.com/watch?v=ZAua8SoJxIY&t=10s.

Abrami, Leo Michael. *The Jewish Origins of the Lord's Prayer*. https://www.academia.edu/search?utf8=%E2%9C%93&q=The+Jewish+Origins+of+the+Lord%27s+Prayer+Leo+Michel+Abrami.

Adler, Cyrus, and Emil G. Hirsch. "Shemoneh Esreh." In *Jewish Encyclopedia*, 11:271. 1906. https://jewishencyclopedia.com/articles/3318-birkat-ha-minim#anchor3.

Angelfire.com. *The Trinity Delusion*, March 19, 2016. http://www.angelfire.com/space/thegospeltruth/TTD/verses/1timothy3_16.html.

Archive.org. *Talmud Bavli (Babylonian Talmud)*. New York: Random House, 1989. https://archive.org/details/talmudtalmudbavloostei.

Athanasius, *De Sententia Dionysii*. https://www.biblestudytools.com/search/?s=references&q=Athanasius%2C+De+Sententia+Dionysii.

Aviam, Mordechai, and William Scott Green. "The Ancient Synagogue: Public Space in Judaism." In *Judaism from Moses to Muhammed: An Interpretation*, edited by Jacob Neusner et al. Boston: Brill, 2005.

Bacon, Josephine, and Martin Gilbert, eds. *Illustrated Atlas of Jewish Civilization: 4000 Years of History*. London: Quantum, 2009.

Baker, R. A. *How the New Testament Canon Was Formed*. https://www.churchhistory101.com/docs/New-Testament-Canon.pdf.

Bakhmutsky, Evgeny. *Historical Rediscovering of Biblical Leadership Within a Local Church*. Clarks Summit, PA: Baptist Bible Seminary, 2013. https://www.academia.edu/10030480/HISTORICAL_REDISCOVERING_OF_BIBLICAL_LEADERSHIP_WITHIN_A_LOCAL_CHURCH2013.

Barton David. "One Room Schoolhouse - Season 2: Episode 22 - Are we in a Great Awakening?" *YouTube*, Apr 28, 2021. https://www.youtube.com/watch?v=HEN-9ngBk2Q.

Belmonte, Vincenzo. *You are Gods at the Origins of Christianity*. https://www.academia.edu/42847396/You_Are_Gods_At_the_Origins_of_Christianity. 2017.

Ben-David, Yirmiyahu. *Who Are the N'tzarim?* San Jose, CA: Schueller, 1994.

Bibliography

Berean Patriot. "The Johannine Comma of 1 John 5:7–8: Added or Removed?" *Berean Patriot*, March 8, 2018. http://www.bereanpatriot.com/the-johannine-comma-of-1-john-57-8-added-or-removed/.

Bibliowicz, Abel Mordechai, *Jewish-Christian Relations: The First Centuries*. Mascarat, 2016. https://abelbibliowicz.academia.edu/research#papers.

Black, Henry Campbell. *Black's Law Dictionary*. 5th ed. St. Paul, MN: West, 1979.

Blue Letter Bible. *Searchable Online Bible with Study Resources*. www.blueletterbible.org.

Boyerin, Daniel. "Justin Martyr Invents Judaism." *Church History* 70.3 (2001) 427–61.

Brennan, Joe. *Basic Principles of Contract Interpretation*. Calgary, AB: Nerland Lindsey, 2015.

Brown, Laurence B. *Misgod'ed: A Roadmap of Guidance and Misguidance Within the Abrahamic Religions*. https://www.academia.edu/9916228/MisGod_ed_laurence_brown. 2007.

Bullinger, E. W. *The Companion Bible*. Reprint, London: Samuel Bagster & Sons, 1970.

———. *Figures of Speech Used in the Bible*. London: Messers. Eyre and Spottiswoode, 1898.

———. "The Hope of Resurrection." *Things to Come* no. 97 9.1 (1902). http://www.teleiosministries.com/HOPE-OF-RESURRECTION.HTML.

———. *Witness of the Stars, the*. Kregel, 1894.

Buzzard, Sir Anthony. Facebook post August 8, 2020. https://www.facebook.com/anthony.buzzard1/posts/10160058065624409.

Buzzard, Sir Anthony, and Charles F. Hunting. *The Doctrine of the Trinity: Christianity's Self-Inflicted Wound*. Morrow, GA: Atlanta Bible College and Restoration Fellowship, 1994.

Cadbury, Henry J. *The Cause and Cure of Modernization,* in *The Historical Jesus in Recent Research*, edited by Dunn et al. University Park, PA: Eisenbrauns, 2005.

Carlson, Kristofer. *Hidden in Plain Sight: Protestants and the Apocrypha, Part I The Development of the Canon*. Norfolk, VA: Dormiton, 2019. https://www.academia.edu/38285305/The_Development_of_the_Canon_docx.

Chabad. *Jewish Stories–From the Midrash*. https://www.chabad.org/library/article_cdo/aid/448345/jewish/Choni-the-Circle-Maker.htm.

Chilton, Bruce, and Jacob Neusner. *Judaism in the New Testament: Practices and Beliefs,* New York: Routledge 1995.

Chilton, Bruce. *Rabbi Jesus: An Intimate Biography*. New York: Doubleday, 2000.

Christian Hospitality. "Myth of Erasmus' Back Translating." *Christian Hospitality* www.christianhospitality.org. undated. https://www.christianhospitality.org/wp/sdm_downloads/great-bible-text-fraud/.

Cloud, David. *What About Erasmus?* Port Huron, MI: Way of Life Literature, 2005.

Bibliography

Costa, Jose. "Some Remarks about Non-Rabbinic Judaism, Rabbinization, and Synagogal Judaism." *Cambridge Semitic Languages and Cultures* 8. Cambridge, UK: Open Book, 2021. https://doi.org/10.11647/OBP.0219.

Cunningham, Jim C., ed. *Nudity & Christianity*. Bloomington, IN: AuthorHouse, 2006.

Dadang, Mipo E. *Christianity: Footprints of the Founding Fathers*. 2nd ed. 2004. https://www.academia.edu/39854820/Christianity_Footprints_of_the_Founding_Fathers.

Davidoff, Benjamin P. "The Ancient Synagogue as Sardis: Religious Pluralism in the Late Roman Empire." *Bowdoin Journal of Art* (2018).

Davis, Adam. "The Logos of Philo and John: A Comparative Sketch." *Blogos: Blogging God's Word*, nd. https://www.blogos.org/churchhistory/philo-logos.php.

Davis, Andrew. "Development of the Doctrine of the Trinity." *Contramodalism*, July 7, 2019. https://contramodalism.com/2019/07/02/the-development-of-the-doctrine-of-the-trinity/.

Davis, R'Menachem. *Perkei Avos – The Artscroll Series*, Brooklyn, NY: Mesorah, 2002.

de la Salle, Pierre. *The Transformation of Jesus, A Voluntary and Disputed Transformation*. 3rd ed. Schleswig-Holstein, Germany: Books on Demand, 2020. https://www.academia.edu/41757463/The_Transformation_of_Jesus_A_voluntary_and_disputed_Transformation.

DeWeese, Chris. "Exegesis of Romans 3: How to Study One of Paul's Letters." *The Word and the Way*, December 22, 2020. https://www.thewordandtheway.net/exegesis-of-romans-3-how-to-study-one-of-pauls-letters/.

Dillenberger, John. *Revelational Discernment and the Problem of the Two Testaments*. In *The Old Testament and Christian Faith*, edited by Bernhard Anderson. New York: Herder & Herder, 1969.

Dostal, Peter J. *Principles of Interpretation*. Halifax, NS: Peter Dostal 2020.

Dunn, James D. G. *Did the First Christians Worship Jesus?* Louisville, KY: Westminster John Knox, 2010.

Edwards, James R. *The Hebrew Gospel and the Development of the Synoptic Tradition*. Grand Rapids, MI: Eerdmans, 2009.

Ehrman, Bart D. *Misquoting Jesus: The Story Behind Who Changed the Bible and Why*. San Francisco: Harper Collins, 2005.

———. *Lost Christianities: The Battles for Scripture and the Faiths We Never Knew*. New York: Oxford University Press, 2003.

Emlyn, Thomas. *A Short Argument, Concerning the Deity of Our Lord Jesus Christ*. London: John Darcy, 1702. http://www.teleiosministries.com/pdfs/New_Articles/An_Humble_Inquiry_into_the_Deity_of_Jesus_Christ.pdf.

Encyclopedia Britanica. *Racovian Catechism*. https://www.britannica.com/topic/Racovian-Catechism.

Bibliography

Erasmus, Desiderius. *New Testament*. 3rd ed. 1522. https://www.originalbibles.com/erasmus-new-testament-1522-third-edition-greek-and-latin-pdf-part-2/.

Errico, Rocco A. *Treasures from the Language of Jesus*. Camarillo, CA: Devorss, 1987.

Essoe, Raymond James. *Shaliah: Introduction to the Law of Agency*. http://www.christianmonotheism.com/media/text/Raymond%20Essoe%20--%20Shaliah.pdf.

Falk, Harvey. *Jesus the Pharisee: A New Look at the Jewishness of Jesus*. Mahwah, NJ: Paulist, 2003.

Finkel, Asher. *Yavneh's Liturgy and Early Christianity*. South Orange, NJ: Seton Hall University, 1981.

Fredriksen, Paula. *Jesus of Nazareth, King of the Jews: A Jewish Life and the Emergence of Christianity*. New York: Alfred A. Knopf, 1999.

Gaston, Thomas Edmund. *Proto-Trinity: The Development of the Doctrine of the Trinity in the First and Second Christian Centuries*. University of Birmingham, 2007. https://www.academia.edu/215530/Proto_Trinity_the_development_of_the_doctrine_of_the_Trinity_in_the_first_and_second_Christian_centuries.

Gathercole, Simon. "Early Christianity - Editorial." *Early Christianity* 6 (2015). https://www.mohrsiebeck.com/en/journal/early-christianity-ec.

Gathercole, Simon. "The Historical and Human Existence of Jesus in Paul's Letters." *Journal for the Study of the Historical Jesus* 16 (2018) 183–212. https://brill.com/view/journals/jshj/16/2-3/article-p183_183.xml.

Gertoux, Gerard. *Did Jesus Know God's Name?* Gerard Geroux, 2017. https://www.academia.edu/33873583/Did_Jesus_Je_HoVaH_salvation_know_God_s_name.

———. *God's Name: Readable but Unpronounceable, Why?* https://www.academia.edu/10728293/Gods_name_readable_but_unpronounceable_why.

Gibbon, Edward. *History of Christianity*. 1776. Reprint, New York: Peter Eckler, 1919. https://archive.org/details/historychristia00gibbgoog/page/n32/mode/2up.

González, Justo L. The *Story of Christianity Volume 1: The Early Church to the Dawn of the Reformation*. 2nd ed. New York: HarperCollins, 2014.

Gordon, Nehemia, and Keith Johnson. *Hebrew Gospel Pearls, Episode 5*. https://www.nehemiaswall.com/hebrew-gospel-pearls-5.

Gordon, Nehemia. "Aviv Barley in the Biblical Calendar." *Nehemia's Wall*, February 24, 2016. https://www.nehemiaswall.com/aviv-barley-in-the-biblical-calendar.

———. *The Hebrew Yeshua vs the Greek Jesus*. Atacosa, TX: Hilkiah, 2005.

———. *Shattering the Conspiracy of Silence: The Hebrew Power of the Priestly Blessing Unleashed*. Atacosa, TX: Hilkiah, 2012.

Green, Steven. *The Apostles' Doctrine Examined*. Wentzville, MO: Urshan Graduate School of Theology, 2017.

Bibliography

Greenberg, Blu. *How to Run a Traditional Jewish Household*. New York: Simon & Schuster, 1983.

Gruell, Tibor. *Reading of the Torah in the First Century Synagogue-New Archaeological Proofs*. Budapest: Gabbiano, 2018. https://www.academia.edu/37544380/Reading_of_the_Torah_in_the_First_Century_Synagogue_New_Archaeological_Proofs.

Haidt, Jonathan. *The Righteous Mind: Why Good People Are divided about Politics and Religion*. New York: Vintage, 2018.

Hamp, Douglas. *Discovering the Language of Jesus*. Santa Ana, CA: Calvary Chapel, 2005.

Hanson, Anthony Tyrrell. *The Image of the Invisible God*. London: SCM, 1982.

Heaton, Robert D. *Teaching Heresy: Lessons from a Critical, Reconstructive Investigation into the Beliefs, Practices and Patristic Refutations of the Ebionites*. Anderson, IN: Anderson University School of Theology, 2013.

Hill, Gary. *History of Religion: The First 500 Years*. Springville, UT: Horizon, 2013. https://www.academia.edu/5699778/A_History_of_Religion_The_First_500_Years.

Hopkins, Richard R. *How Greek Philosophy Corrupted the Christian Concept of God*. Horizon, 2009.

Horrell, David G. "Early Jewish Christianity." In *The Early Christian World*, edited by P. F. Esler, vol. 1. London: Routledge, 2000. https://www.academia.edu/6185652/Early_Jewish_Christianity?sm=b.

———. "The Label Xristianos: 1 Peter 4:6 and the Formation of Christian Identity." *Journal of Biblical Literature* 126.2 (2007) 361–81. https://www.academia.edu/6266507/The_Label_Xristiano_j_1_Pet_4_16_and_the_Formation_of_Christian_Identity?sm=b.

———. *Pauline Churches or Early Christian Churches? Unity, Disagreement, and the Eucharist*. University of Exeter, 2008. https://www.academia.edu/6102543/Pauline_Churches_or_Early_Christian_Churches_Unity_Disagreement_and_the_Eucharist?sm=b.

———. "Whose Faith(fulness) Is It in 1 Peter 1:5?" *The Journal of Theological Studies* 48.1 (1997) 110–15. https://www.academia.edu/6267716/Whose_faith_fulness_is_it_in_1_Peter_1_5?sm=b.

Howard, George. *Hebrew Gospel of Matthew*. Macon, GA: Mercer University Press, 1995.

Huggins, Hal A. *It's All in Your Head: The Link between Mercury Amalgams and Illness*. New York: Penguin, 1993.

Hylton, Antony Michael. *"Jesus Is Lord" in the Christ Hymn of Philippians 2:9–11 in Its First Century Jewish Context*. https://www.academia.edu/37801952/_Jesus_is_Lord_in_the_Christ_hymn_of_Philippians_2_9_11_in_its_first_century_Jewish_Context, 2011.

Irons, Charles Lee, et al. *The Son of God: Three Views of the Identity of Jesus*. Eugene, OR: Wipf & Stock, 2015.

Bibliography

Islamic Awareness. "Early Lists of The Books of The New Testament." *Islamic Awareness*, 1999. https://www.islamic-awareness.org/bible/text/canon/canonlists.html#1.

Jacomb-Hood, Anthony. *Rediscovering the New Testament Church*. New York, NY: CreateSpace, 2014. https://rediscoveringthentchurch.com/download/619/.

Johnson, Keith E. *His Hallowed Name Revealed Again*. Charlotte, NC: Biblical Foundations Academy, 2010.

Jones, Miles. *Sons of Zion vs Sons of Greece: Volume One: Survival of the Hebrew Gospels and the Messianic Church*. Kerrville, TX: Benei Emunah Institute, 2019.

Justin Martyr. *Dialog with Trypho the Jew, § LXVII*. Translated by A. Lukin Williams. New York: Society for Promoting Christian Knowledge, MacMillan, 1930.

Keenan, Daniel. *Transmission of the Apostles' Doctrine, Written and Oral: How Is the Apostles' Teaching Passed On?* Victoria, BC: Daniel Keeran, nd. https://www.academia.edu/19890782/Transmission_of_the_Apostles_Doctrine.

Keiser, Lewis. *The Pre-Christian Teachings of Yeshua*. https://www.academia.edu/11318607/THE_PRE-CHRISTIAN_TEACHINGS_OF_YESHUA?email_work_card=view-paper%20p14.

Kenyon, E. W. *The Blood Covenant*. Lynnwood, WA: Kenyon's Gospel Publishing Society, 1969.

Kinzig, Wolfram. "The Nazoraeans." In *Jewish Believers in Jesus*, edited by Oskar Skarsaune and Reidar Hvalik, 463–87. Peabody, MA: Hendrickson, 2007. https://www.academia.edu/36508014/The_Nazoraeans.

KJV Today. *Johannine Comma (1 John 5:7)*. http://www.kjvtoday.com/home/the-father-the-word-and-the-holy-ghost-in-1-john-57?tmpl=%2Fsystem%2Fapp%2Ftemplates%2Fprint%2F&showPrintDialog=1.

Kuhn, Thomas S. *The Structure of Scientific Revolutions*. 3rd ed. Chicago: University of Chicago Press, 1996.

Lamsa, George. *The New Testament from the Ancient Eastern Text*. New York: HarperCollins, 1989. http://www.superbook.org/LAMSA/LK/lk3.htm.

Law, Steve. "New Discoveries Indicate Hebrew Was World's Oldest Alphabet, Parts 1–3." *Patterns of Evidence* January 6–19, 2017. https://patternsofevidence.com/2017/01/06/new-discoveries-indicate-hebrew-was-worlds-oldest-alphabet/.

Levine, Lee I, *The Ancient Synagogue, the First Thousand Years*. New Haven, CT: Yale University Press, 2005.

Liebowitz, Etka. "Hypocrites or Pious Scholars? The Image of the Pharisees in Second Temple Period Texts and Rabbinic Literature," *Melilah Manchester Journal of Jewish Studies* 11 (2014) 53–67. http://static1.1.sqspcdn.com/static/f/784513/26059114/1426785793110/4.pdf?token=DDUIWJUdRrlR8ax71%2FPWGkxW1iE%3D.

Lipsitt, Amanda. *The Secret Society: Descendants of Crypto-Jews in the San Antonia Area*. San Antonio, TX: University of Texas Press, 2007. https://

Bibliography

www.academia.edu/24532929/The_Secret_Society_Descendants_of_Crypto_Jews_in_the_San_Antonio_Area.

Litwa, M. David. "You Are Gods: Deification in the Naassene Writer and Clement of Alexandria." *Harvard Theological Review* 110.1 (2017) 125–48. https://www.cambridge.org/core/journals/harvard-theological-review/article/you-are-gods-deification-in-the-naassene-writer-and-clement-of-alexandria/C80F703545F874BFF70612BFC1D92021.

Locke, John. *The Reasonableness of Christianity*. London: Awnsham and John Churchill, 1695. The Online Library of Liberty. http://oll.libertyfund.org.

Magee, D. M. "Christianity Revealed: Judaism and the Jewish Sects." *AskWhy!*, 2003. http://www.askwhy.co.uk/christianity/AW_a2_Christianity.pdf

Mamatha. "Jesus: I Am the Burning Bush." *Living Room Theology*, November 12, 2018. https://livingroomtheology.com/jesus-i-am-the-burning-bush.

Marlowe, Michael D. "The Johannine Comma." *The Bible Researcher*, nd. http://www.bible-researcher.com/comma.html.

Martorana, Vincent R. *A Guide to Contract Interpretation*. Pittsburgh, PA: Reed Smith, 2014. https://www.reedsmith.com/files/uploads/miscellany/A_Guide_to_Contract_Interpretation__July_2014_.pdf.

McCuiston, Paul R. *Development of the Concept and Practice of Ordination in the New Testament and the Early Church*. Johnson Bible College. 2009.

McDonald's. "Israeli Mcdonald's Commerical." *YouTube*, July 1, 2008. https://www.youtube.com/watch?v=CFT8cW8YNZ0.

McDowell, Gavin, et al., eds. *Diversity and Rabbinization: Jewish Texts and Societies Between 400 and 1,000 CE*. Cambridge, UK: Open Book, 2021. https://doi.org/10.11647/OBP.0219.

McGrath, Alister E. *Historical Theology: An Introduction to the History of Christian Thought*. 2nd ed. Oxford: John Wiley & Sons, 2013.

McGrath, James F. *The Only True God: Early Christian Monotheism in its Jewish Context*. University of Illinois Press, 2009.

Meeks, Wayne A. *The First Urban Christians: The Social World of the Apostle Paul*. New Haven, CT: Yale University Press, 1983.

Meir, Asher. "Wearing and Tying Shoes." *Meaning in Mitzvot*, nd. https://outorah.org/p/20623.

Mendes, A. P. *The Daily Prayers*. London: P. Valentine, 1864.

Meyers, Robin. *Spiritual Defiance: Building a Beloved Community of Resistance*. New Haven, CT: Yale University Press, 2015.

My Jewish Learning. "Jewish Resurrection of the Dead: When and How Will the Dead Be Brought Back to Life?" *My Jewish Learning*, nd. https://www.myjewishlearning.com/article/jewish-resurrection-of-the-dead/.

———. "Kashrut & Reform Judaism." *My Jewish Learning*, undated. https://www.myjewishlearning.com/article/article/kashrut-reform-judaism/.

———. "Shower on Shabbat: Can I Rinse Off on the Holy Day?" *Ask the Expert*. https://www.myjewishlearning.com/article/ask-the-expert-shower-on-shabbat/.

Bibliography

Nessim, Daniel F. J. *Didache and Trinity: Proto-Trinitarianism in an Early Christian Community.* San Antonio, TX: Daniel F. J. Nessim, 2016. https://www.academia.edu/30354503/Didache_and_Trinity_Proto_Trinitarianism_in_an_Early_Christian_Community.

Neusner, Jacob, and Alan J. Avery-Peck. *The Blackwell Companion to Judaism.* Malden, MA: Blackwell, 2003.

New Scientist. "Vatican Admits Galileo Was Right." *New Scientist*, November 7, 1992. https://www.newscientist.com/article/mg13618460-600-vatican-admits-galileo-was-right/.

New Testament Christians. "351 Old Testament Prophecies Fulfilled in Jesus Christ." *New Testament Christians*, nd. https://www.newtestamentchristians.com/bible-study-resources/351-old-testament-prophecies-fulfilled-in-jesus-christ/.

One God Worship. "How Plato Influenced Our View of God." *One God Worship*, August 12, 2019. https://onegodworship.com/how-plato-influenced-our-view-of-god/.

———. "The Principle of Agency in the New Testament." *One God Worship*, July 9, 2019. https://onegodworship.com/the-principle-of-agency-in-the-new-testament/.

The Open Siddur Project. "Abbreviated Blessing After the Meal." *The Open Siddur Project*. https://opensiddur.org/prayers/eating/birkat-hamazon/blessing-the-spirit-of-life-after-eating-and-feeling-satiated/.

Paine, Levi Leonard. *A Critical History of the Evolution of Trinitarianism and its Outcome in the New Christology.* New York: Houghton Mifflin, 1900.

Pillai, K C. *Light Through an Eastern Window.* New York: Robert Speller & Sons, 1963.

———. *Orientalisms in the Bible, vol 1.* Fairborn, OH: Minkus, 1969.

Priestley, Joseph. *An History of the Corruptions of Christianity in Two Volumes.* Birmingham, UK: Percy & Jones, 1782. https://archive.org/details/anhistorycorrupo1priegoog.

Pritz, Ray A. *Nazarene Jewish Christianity from the End of the New Testament Period Until Its Disappearance in the Fourth Century.* Jerusalem: Magnes, 1992.

Psychology Today Staff. "Dunning-Kruger Effect." *Psychology Today*, August 12, 2019. https://www.psychologytoday.com/us/basics/dunning-kruger-effect.

Reeves, Ryan M. "Church History's Greatest Myths: Erasmus and the Greek New Testament." *Reformation21*, February 8, 2016. https://www.reformation21.org/articles/church-historys-greatest-myths.php.

Richardson, Joel. *Sinai to Zion: The Untold Story of the Triumphant Return of Jesus.* Leawood, KS: Winepress, 2021.

Robinson, Shirley J. *Online Greek Textbook.* Clovis, NM: Shirley J. Robinson, 2011. http://www.drshirley.org/greek/textbook/.

Rohl, David M. *Pharaohs and Kings: A Biblical Quest.* New York: Crown, 1995.

Rood, Michael. *The Chronological Gospels,* Charlotte, NC: Aviv Moon, 2013.

Bibliography

Roth, Wolfgang. *Hebrew Gospel: Cracking the Code of Mark*. Eugene, OR: Wipf & Stock, 2009.

Runesson, Anders. *Nature and Origin of the 1st-Century Synagogue*. McMaster University, Canada, 2004.

Safrai, Shmuel. "The Place of Women in First-century Synagogues." *Priscilla Papers*, Winter 2002. https://www.academia.edu/35099564/The_Place_of_Women_in_First_century_Synagogues_They_were_much_more_active_in_religious_life_than_they_are_today.

Sanders, E. P. *Common Judaism and the Synagogue in the First Century*. https://www.academia.edu/11867081/Common_Judaism_and_the_synagogue_in_the_first_century.

Schaff, Philip. *History of the Christian Church, the*. New York: Charles Scribner's Sons, 1889. https://archive.org/details/historyofchristo1scha.

Scherman, Nosson. *The Complete Artscroll Siddur*. New York: Mesorah, 1985.

Schiffman, Lawrence H. *From Text to Tradition: A History of Second Temple Judaism*. Hoboken, NJ: Ktav, 1991.

Shapiro, Mark Dov. *Gates of Shabbat: A Guide for Observing Shabbat*. New York, NY: Central Conference of American Rabbis, 1996.

Shurpin, Yehudah: "Why Isn't Poultry and Dairy Kosher?" *Chabad*, July 1, 2020. https://www.chabad.org/library/article_cdo/aid/4788772/jewish/Why-Isnt-Poultry-and-Dairy-Kosher.htm#utm_medium=email&utm_source=1_chabad.org_magazine_en&utm_campaign=en&utm_content=content.

Sichel, Matthew S. *Evaluating Postmissionary Messianic Judaism: Authority, Christology and the Church of God*. Evangelical Theological Seminary, 2019. https://www.academia.edu/39125015/Evaluating_Postmissionary_Messianic_Judaism_Authority_Christology_and_the_Church_of_God 2019.

Silberberg, Naftali. "Why Is the Shofar Not Blown on Shabbat?" *Chabad*, December, 20, 2020. https://www.chabad.org/library/article_cdo/aid/988699/jewish/Why-No-Shofar-on-Shabbat.htm.

Sondergarrd, Torben. *The Last Reformation: Back to the New Testament Model of Discipleship*. McDonough, GA: Laurus, 2013.

Sperber, Daniel. "Congregational Dignity and Human Dignity: Women and Public Torah Reading." *The Edah Journal* 3.2 (2003) Elul 5763.

Spirit and Truth Fellowship, International. *Revised English Version*. Bloomington, IN: Spirit and Truth Fellowship, International, 2014. https://www.revisedenglishversion.com/.

Stanford University. "History of Trinitarian Doctrines." *Stanford Encyclopedia of Philosophy*. https://plato.stanford.edu/entries/trinity/trinity-history.html.

Stark, Rodney. *The Rise of Christianity*, San Francisco: HarperCollins, 1997.

Stimson, Dorothy. *The Gradual Acceptance of the Copernican Theory of the Universe*. New York: Baker & Taylor, 1917. https://www.gutenberg.org/files/35744/35744-h/35744-h.htm, 2011.

Bibliography

Strong, James and John McClintock. "Trinity." *Encyclopaedia of Biblical, Theological, and Ecclesiastical Literature*, Vol. 10. New York: Harper, 1891.

Strong, James. *The Exhaustive Concordance of the Bible*. Nashville, TN: Abingdon, 1894.

Sungenis, Robert A. *Not By Scripture Alone: A Catholic Critique of the Protestant Doctrine of Sola Scriptura*. State Line, PA: Catholic Apologetics International, 2013. https://www.academia.edu/36443121/NOT_BY_SCRIPTURE_ALONE_A_Catholic_Critique_of_the_Protestant_Doctrine_of_Sola_Scriptura_Second_edition.

Suter, John Wallace, ed. *The Book of Common Prayer*. New York: Seabury, 1953.

Teileios Ministries. *Spirit and Soul (Recognizing Inherent flaws in our Bible Translations)*. http://teleiosministries.com/spiritofyahweh.html.

The Watchman Fellowship, inc. *Index of Cults and Religions*. https://www.watchman.org/index-of-cults-and-religions/#Christianity.

Theopedia. "Johannine Comma." *An Encyclopedia of Biblical Christianity*, undated. https://www.theopedia.com/johannine-comma.

Trumbull, H. Clay. *Blood Covenant, the*. New York: Impact, 1975.

Van Noort, Ben. "Who appeared to Moses at the Burning Bush?" *Contradicting Bible Contradictions*. https://www.contradictingbiblecontradictions.com/?p=528, 2011.

Vasileiadis, Pavlos, and Nehemia Gordon. "Transmission of the Tetragrammaton in Judeo-Greek and Christian Sources." *Cahiers Accademia* 12 (2021) 85–126. https://www.academia.edu/38634875/_Transmission_of_the_Tetragrammaton_in_Judeo_Greek_and_Christian_SourcesΜεταβίβαση_του_Τετραγράμματου_ στις_Ιουδαιο_Ελληνικές_και_Χριστιανικές_Πηγές_Cahiers_Accademia_Nr_12_June_2021_pp_85_126.

Ware, Henry, Jr. *Outline of the Testimony of Scripture Against the Trinity*. Boston: Charles Bowen, 1832. https://babel.hathitrust.org/cgi/pt?id=ien.35556001718519&view=1up&seq=7.

Weinberg, Steven. *To Explain the World: The Discovery of Modern Science*. New York: Harper, 2015.

Wenstrom, William E., Jr. *Exegesis and Exposition of First Thessalonians* 1:1. Marion, IA: William E. Wenstrom, Jr. Bible Ministries, 2018. https://www.academia.edu/40286140/Exegesis_and_Exposition_of_First_Thessalonians_1_1.

———. *God the Son Revisited*. Marion, IA: William E. Wenstrom, Jr. Bible Ministries 2014. https://www.academia.edu/40286140/Exegesis_and_Exposition_of_First_Thessalonians_1_1.

Whiston, William. *An Account of the Faith of the First Two Centuries*. William Whiston, 1711. http://www.teleiosministries.com/pdfs/john%20locke/Faithof%20the%20first%20two%20centuries.pdf.

White, Benjamin L. "'The Eschatological Conversion of All the Nations' in Matthew 28:19-20: (Mis)reading Matthew through Paul." *Journal for the Study of the New Testament*. Journal for the Study of the New Testament 36.4 (2014) 353–82.

Bibliography

Wierwille, V. P. *Jesus Christ Is Not God.* New Knoxville, OH: American Christian, 1975.

Wilbur, Earl Morse. *A History of Unitarianism Socinianism and its Antecedents.* Harvard University Press, 1945.

Wilson, Jake. *A Few Remarks on the Trinity: The Forgery of Matthew* 28:19. https://www.researchgate.net/publication/350957224_THE_ANTI-SEMITIC_FORGERY_OF_MATTHEW_2819. April, 2021.

Wilson, Marvin R. *Our Father Abraham: Jewish Roots of the Christian Faith.* Grand Rapids, MI: William B. Eerdmans, 1989.

Wink, Walter. *Engaging the Powers: Discernment and Resistance in a World of Domination.* Minneapolis, MN: Fortress, 1992.

Woods, David B. *Jews and Gentiles in the Ecclesia: Evaluating the Theory of Intra-Ecclesial Jew-Gentile Distinction.* South African Theological Seminary, 2005.

Young, Brad D. *Jesus the Jewish Theologian.* Peabody, MA: Hendrickson, 1995.

Zarley, Kermit. *The Real Jesus.* Kermit Zarley, 2011. http://servetustheevangelical.com/doc/TheRealJesus_tract.pdf.

———. *The Restitution of Jesus Christ.* Kermit Zarley, 2008. http://servetustheevangelical.com/restitution_of_jesus_christ_1.html.

Zahavy, Zvee. "Tractate Talmud Baba Mezi'a 59b." *Babylonian Talmud.* https://halakhah.com/babamezia/babamezia_59.html#PARTb.

Zaslow, David, and Joseph Lieberman. *Jesus: First Century Rabbi.* Orleans, MA: Paraclete, 2014.

Zaslow, David. "TBT Humble Texas with Rabbi David Zaslow and his Jesus: First Century Rabbi." *YouTube,* June 25, 2020. https://www.youtube.com/watch?v=E4gqL6c5U84.

www.ingramcontent.com/pod-product-compliance
Lightning Source LLC
Chambersburg PA
CBHW072135160426
43197CB00012B/2122